The God-Kings of Europe

The Descendents of Jesus Traced Through the Odonic and Davidic Dynasties

Hugh Montgomery

The Book Tree
San Diego, CA

The God-Kings of Europe
© 2006
Hugh Montgomery

ISBN 978-1-58509-109-6

Library of Congress Control Number: 2006928908

Cover layout and design
Atulya Berube

Printed on Acid-Free Paper
in the United States and United Kingdom
by LightningSource, Inc.

Published by
The Book Tree
P O Box 16476
San Diego, CA 92176

We provide fascinating and educational products to help awaken the public to new ideas and information that would not be available otherwise.
Call 1 (800) 700-8733 for our *FREE BOOK TREE CATALOG*.

Table of Contents

ILLUSTRATIONS

CHARTS and DOCUMENTS

Acknowledgments

Although this book is my work, many friends and colleagues have helped me. I have to thank two people in particular. The first is my distant cousin Sophie Montgomery of Sweden. She made available to me not only her late father's published work but allowed me full access to his library and notes. Without Dr. Bo-Gabriel Montgomery's careful research into the early migrations and Gothic kings I would not have been able to write this book. In particular, his knowledge of Old Norse was invaluable. His work deserves to be much more widely known. The second is Dr. Yuri Stoyanov, Golda Meir Professor of comparative religions at the Hebrew University, Jerusalem and Director of the British Archaeological studies in the Levant. He is the world's leading authority on the Hidden Tradition in Europe and his knowledge of the Elchasaites, Cathars and Bogomils is unrivalled. He has not only made several suggestions to me as to sources but has given me unstintingly of his time and expertise. I must also thank Dr. Margaret Tottle-Smith for the use of her researches in France and the Map she drew. Also, the curators and owners of many of the collections of documents, in particular the Chief Archivist of the Danish Royal Archives, who sent me, free of charge, copies of documents which I have used and the Mayor of Bellême, who allowed my wife and I unfettered access to the Library during a time when it is normally closed. I must also thank the Headmaster of the Royal Grammar School, Guildford, who allowed me access to the school's wonderful collection of early religious texts, in particular, the Polyglot Bible with its Syrian and Chaldean texts of Mathew and John. Special thanks must go to Major Niven Sinclair, Chairman of the Clan Sinclair Trust, who has sent me copies of documents belonging to the trust—some of which are now in the Bodleian. To the Norris Collection and its Archivist, Jim Gerencser, who allowed me to use their front piece of Abdias and who kindly allowed me copies of this document. Some of the documents used or referenced are in private collections whose owners have preferred to remain anonymous. Your wishes will be adhered to, but you nonetheless have my thanks. To Maria Hearl, for her researches in Cyprus and Tyatira, her translations of Greek, and the photographs of original documents. The Bruce Family, for trawling the Tischendorf Collection in Glasgow and particularly for all the work on the Ante-Nicaean Fathers and

Tischendorf's commentary on Abdias. To all the academics around the world in the USA, Canada, Russia, Serbia, Denmark, the Netherlands and the UK, who have answered all my queries patiently and provided me with their expertise free of charge, my grateful thanks. There are probably many others whom I should mention and who have helped me over the years. Please accept my thanks if I have inadvertently not mentioned you. I must also thank my agent Jennifer Solignac and my publisher for the speed with which they have acted, and last but not least my wife, Hermione, who has had to put up with my bad temper when things do not go according to plan, who reminds me to eat when I am busy working, who keeps my feet on the ground when I am on a high and picks me up when I am low. Your love sustains me.

About the Author

Professor Hugh Montgomery retired two years ago as President of the Megatrend University of Applied Sciences in Belgrade, where he lectured on History, Politics and Economics. Prior to becoming a full time academic, Hugh Montgomery had a successful business career in South America, Africa, the Middle East and the UK.

He holds a Ph.D. in Audiology, a Diploma in Contract Law and the professional qualification of Inginiero Comercial (Chile). He is the author of a number of technical and historical papers and books including: *Montgomery Millennium, The Norman Families and the Conquest of England* (a Ph.D. thesis submitted to the University in Belgrade), *Industrial Hearing Conservation in South Africa, Audiometric Calibration and Jet Engine Fault Diagnosis using a Scanning Electron Microscope and E.D.X.* He was a Founding Fellow of the Institution of Diagnostic Engineers. He has given a number of talks and interviews on both radio and television in Belgrade, South Africa and the UK.

He speaks Spanish and German and was recently elected a Fellow of the prestigious Society of Antiquaries of Scotland—Scotland's oldest learned Society, going back to 1780. He lives in Uttoxeter with his wife Hermione.

Chapter 1

The Odonic Line

Once upon a time in a land far away called Mesopotamia there was a king so wise, so powerful, that his subjects decided he must be a God. His name was Uôuin. However, this is not a fairy tale, but history.

I propose during this book to take the reader on a voyage of historical discovery and equally one of detection as we piece together bits of an historical jigsaw puzzle to come up with some surprising answers. At the same time, I have tried to make the book as academically rigorous as is possible when dealing with information that is mostly many hundreds of years old.

Uôuin means "Lord" in Aryan or "The One", and is the same as the Hebrew "Adonai" or, in Kassite, Iddina or Agum. In the Nordic languages it is most commonly Woden, Odin or Wotan and from now on I shall use the name Odin as being most familiar to us.

The name Uôuin (probably pronounced like the Scots name Ewen), was not in fact the name of one particular king, but was part of the name of a number of Babylonian kings from the Kassite dynasty onwards (1595 BC–1157 BC). Indeed, it may well pre-date the Babylonian Empire to that of Sumeria. Louise Hamilton's recent article "Outline of the Nature of Sumerian Gods and their Relationship with their 'Home' Cities", gives a fascinating glimpse into the way these Gods were viewed by the Sumerians and those who followed them. "Sumerian gods were envisaged in human shape and were considered to have the same basic needs. Cult statues were the vehicles through which the gods manifested themselves on earth.... imbued with...the divine presence."[1] If a city fell it was because the God had left.

There is evidence to suggest that Odin or Uôuin is based upon An/Anu, the leader of the assembly of Gods and God of the Sky in Sumerian mythology who, together with the female deity Ishtar/Inanna, was the patron deity of the city of Uruk.[2] We dismiss these ideas at our peril. Remember that many of the Jewish/Christian myths in the Bible can be found to have their origins in Sumerian legends, the story of the flood being an obvious one. It is worthwhile noting at this point that Anu would be Ian in Gaelic and John in English,

9

and that Inanna becomes Joanna, Hanah or Anna and that Ishtar is the same as the Hebrew name Esther.

Norse mythology betrays a remarkable Sumerian influence and there is a strong tradition linking the Royal pedigrees of the Scandinavian kings to the ancient kingdoms of Asia Minor. The words Sumer, Sumerii, Sumeriana, Gumer, Gumner and possibly Gomari all appear to refer to the Sumerians. In the Icelandic epic *Hyndlujóo* there is a passage which reads in translation: "But Randver was, Radbard's son, those Gumer were blessed by the Gods" (peir uóru gumnar gopum signapir).

In several of the old manuscripts the last two lines have been deleted, as if the very idea that Odin could have originated in the hot lush pastures of Sumeria, instead of the frozen north, was unimaginable. However, they have been reinserted in the historical chronology known as *Flaterjarbók*.

In the genealogy of the Kings of Mercia their ancestor is called Weoôulgeot, or more correctly, Rhoes the Weoôulgeot. A variation of this name is Weotguigeot, (Uôui or Odingoth or Odin-God). Jutland, in turn, means Uôuin's land; therefore the ruler or chieftain so called would have been clearly showing that he was not only a descendent of Odin, but also ruler of Odin's land.

According to the legends of the Goths, they originated in Southern Sweden in what is now Jutland. Just off the coast of Jutland is a small island still called Gotland. There are also two areas of Sweden called respectively Vastra Gotaland and Ostergotaland (meaning West and East Gotland). From there they moved south into the area between the Oder and Vistula in what is now Poland. Thence they seem to have drifted into the Ukraine and Scythia, but one needs to ask if in fact they were Kassite in origin. Did they migrate originally from Mesopotamia northwards in their wheeled chariots, skirting the Black Sea into the Ukraine and the western steppes, intermarrying on the way and eventually making it to Sweden? Was their very name "Goth", meaning God, a remembrance that once they had been God-Kings in another place? We know for example that they at least made it as far as Gaul (modern France), where they were known as Cassi.[3]

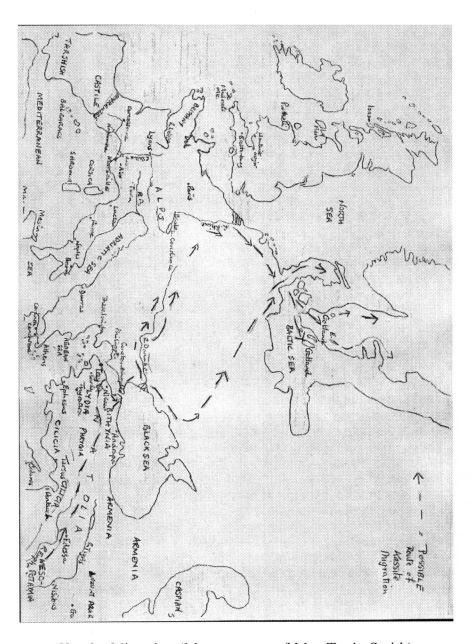

Kassite Migration (Map courtesy of Meg Tottle-Smith)

At least one authority maintains that the Kassites, in Sanskrit Kassu, had held the mountain chain of Pusht-I-Kuh along the south-western coast of the Caspian Sea. From here they had invaded the Sumerian kingdom, initially prior to 2000 BC and then again in 1962 BC, and lastly in 1758 BC when the original Sumerian dynasty was overthrown and the Kassite dynasty took its place. The Kassite dynasty had already established trading links with Europe, particular for tin and copper, and it is not unreasonable to suppose that when their dynasty in Babylon was overthrown in 1157 BC by the Isin dynasty, that the remnants of this people migrated north again. In fact the Spanish Kingdom of Castile is named after one of the great Kassite kings—Kastilias, or Kashtiliashu III, who died in 1483 BC.[4]

Recently some genetic evidence has come to light which seems to confirm my hypothesis that the Goths may have come from Mesopotamia.[5] The genetic mutation CCR5-delta32 has been known to science for some time. According to Prof. Christopher Duncan and Dr. Susan Scott of the University of Liverpool Biology Dept., this mutation first occurred in Mesopotamia near to the Euphrates and Tigris rivers sometime around 1150-1000 BC, exactly the time of the Kassite dynasty's overthrow. This gene is to be found in high levels in Scandinavia but relatively low levels in areas bordering the Mediterranean. This would appear, I suggest, to prove my hypothesis of the Kassite migration!

There is indeed a genealogy which purports to show the descent of Rhoes the Weoôulgeot from the deified kings of Mesopotamia—unfortunately there is no secondary confirmation in any of the old chronicles or literature of Rome, which has come down to us. We must therefore start with Rhoes, the first historically established King of the Visigoths, who flourished at the beginning of the fourth century. He is called Rothesteus or Rhotestes in the *Life of Saint Sabas* (Vit.S. Sabae, Act.SS. Apr. II, 967 D) and the *Orations of Themistics* (Orat. XV. 191 A). Both of these names are a variation of Rhoeteus, which means Trojan. So we may conclude that his origins were from Troy. (Troy was, of course, on the western coast of modern Turkey and on the route northwards from Mesopotamia to Sweden.) In Old Norse his name would have been Rhoes and it is this variation that I am using throughout this book. It is one of the problems to which the reader will have to become accustomed during the course of this book, and that is that many historical figures were called by different names in different languages. Latin scribes in particular Latinised any non-Latin name as they felt best, and often, different scribes Latinised names differently.

Rhoes therefore was claiming descent from the ancient kings of Troy and their Gods, amongst the most important of whom, was the deified King of Mesopotamia, Odin.

Because the most famous account of the Trojan War was written in Greek, many people assume that the Trojans worshipped the same Gods as the Greeks but this was not so. Rhoes was *"the"* Weoôulgeot, which meant Chief of all the Visigoths and Pontiff of Odin in the Germanic world. On more than one occasion his people fought side by side with the Romans and Constantine the Great held him in such high esteem that he raised a statue to him in Constantinople. It is also possible that Rhoes met the great Church historian Eusebius with consequences for his descendents as we shall see in a later chapter.

How did a Visigothic king come to be fighting with the Romans? To answer this we must go back a little in time. The Goths had, as I mentioned, drifted into Scythia but by 238 AD had become a power in their own right. In 238 AD the Gothic Army crossed the Danube and laid waste a considerable amount of Roman land. They retired when they were bought off with vast bribes (similar to Danegeld!).

In 250 AD they invaded again under their King Kniva and this time their army included a large number of Vandals. Philippopolis was sacked and in 251 AD a Roman Army was defeated at Abrittus and the Emperor Decius and his son were killed in the Swamps of Dobrudja. General Gallus made peace with the Goths, bribing them once again not to return.

The Gothic Kingdom lasted until 270 AD when the Roman Emperor Aurelius defeated the Gothic Army and killed their king, Cannabaudes. After this the Goths split into two separate groups—the Tervingi branch, who become known as Visigoths, and the Greutungi branch, which become known as the Ostrogoths.

The Ostrogoths were eventually conquered by the Huns in 372 AD. They became loyal followers of the Huns and formed part of the Army of Attila at the battle of Châlons in 451 AD, where they found themselves fighting against their cousins the Visigoths, who were allies of the Roman Aëtius. The Huns were defeated and Attila himself died in 453 AD. The Romans now persuaded the Ostrogoths, under their king, Theodoric, to move into Italy, establishing the Ostrogothic Kingdom of Italy.

This was the time of the remaining one hundred years of the old Western Roman Empire. The Emperor Diocletian had divided the old Roman Empire into two, the Eastern Empire based on Constantinople or Byzantium, and the Western Roman Empire based upon the old capital city, Rome. In 308 AD Constantine I had reunited the Empire and it was during his reign (308-337 AD) that a statue was put up to Rhoes the Weoôulgeot. When Constantine died the Empire was once again divided and it was not until the time of Theodosius I, known as the Great, who after ruling the Eastern Empire for a while, managed to reunite the two halves. This was not to last. At his death the Empire split once again, never to be reunited.

This was also the time of change from the old multi-faith pagan and classical Roman Empire to the Christianisation of the Empire. Somewhere around 312-313 AD Constantine accepted Christianity, though this date is not supported by all scholars. At all events, in 325 AD Constantine called the Council of Nicaea to decide between the Arian concept of Father and Son being different substances, or the Orthodox doctrine of One Substance. The Council decided on the latter. On the 11th May, 330 AD Constantine dedicated his new capital city of Constantinople, built upon the site of ancient Byzantium. Eusebius was responsible for Constantine reinstating Arius and exiling Anastasius though Anastasius's doctrine of One Substance eventually became the accepted doctrine. By 336 AD the priest Arius was tortured to death for preaching that God and Christ were of different substances. Other religious beliefs were forbidden and pagan temples closed. In order for the Emperor to convert, it was necessary to change the concept of the Romans being responsible for Jesus' death. Obviously Constantine was not going to admit that the Roman Empire had been responsible for the death of the World's Saviour. The Gospels were hastily changed, but the problem was who were they to make responsible for Jesus' death? Eventually the doctrine was devised that because the Jews had not accepted Jesus as the "Heavenly" as opposed to "Earthly" Messiah, that therefore they were responsible. John's Gospel in particular is heavily anti-Semitic and was specifically changed to make out that the Jews were responsible.

One of the more bizarre results of Constantine's acceptance of Christianity was the works of his mother, the Empress Helen. In 328 AD she "discovered" the tomb of Jesus in Jerusalem. Naturally, as the mother of the Emperor, all the priests and others slavishly agreed. I can hear them now, "Of course Your Imperial Majesty—How clever of Your Imperial Majesty—Of course it's the Tomb of Jesus, Your Imperial Majesty." The most amazing thing is, that it is now the "Church of the Holy Sepulchre" and most of the people worshiping at the site have no idea how it was "found". Helen however did not leave it there. She went on to discover the Holy Cross, which she pronounced to be "Green and living". So she had it cut down and divided into four pieces. One piece each was sent to Jerusalem, Rome, Constantinople and Colchester. Today all those "pieces of the true cross", which are venerated in various places, all stem from these. But she was not content with even these two miraculous discoveries; she discovered the *nails of the cruxifiction*. Were they imbedded in the cross, one asks oneself? She later "discovered" the bodies of the three Magi. She was altogether a remarkable lady!! The Church of course made her a Saint and she is the patron Saint of Colchester, whose Coat of Arms recalls these miraculous discoveries.

The Table below shows the Emperors from Constantine I: AD

Constantine I	308-337
Constantine II (Jointly)	337-340
Constans (Jointly)	337-350
Constantius II (Jointly)	337-361
Magnentius (Jointly)	350-353
Julian (the Apostate)	361-363
Jovianus	363-364
Valentinian I (Rules West)	364-375
Valens (Rules East)	364-378
Gratian (Rules West)	375-383
Magnus Maximus (The British Emperor or usurper in West)	383-388
Valentinian II (Rules West)	375-392
Eugenius (Usurper in West)	392-394
Theodosius I (Rules East and unites East and West)	378-395

Meanwhile, between 270-370 AD, the Visigoths had become auxiliaries for the Roman armies and by the time of Rhoes (birth date unknown but probably around 300 AD), they were highly regarded by Constantine I (308-337), notwithstanding that they were worshippers of Odin. However in 376 AD the Romans once again attempted to force the Visigoths, who had settled in Moesia, on the Roman side of the Danube, back across the river. The Visigoths had fled from the Huns and sought refuge with the Romans. Their treatment at the hands of the Romans was so bad, however (see Gibbon, *The Rise and Fall of the Roman Empire*), that in 378 AD, under Alaric and Ataulf, they rose up and utterly defeated a Roman Army under the Emperor Valens at Adrianople. This was the first time that cavalry had been shown to be superior to the old Roman Legions. The Romans now decided they were better friends than enemies and signed a treaty with them in 382 AD. By 400 AD the traditional foot soldiers of Roman Legions had all but disappeared and the auxiliaries or Foederati became the only force of importance within the Western Roman Empire.[6]

When Rhoes died, he was succeeded by his son Athanaric, which is the Gothic form of the Chattic name Hattaric or Chattaric. It is likely that he was the Gothic or Chattic Chieftain of South Jutland, West Germany and the Low Countries. He is mentioned by Saint Jerome and others and is called the "Judge of the Thervingi" or Thuringians. His name in the Mercian pedigree is Uihtlag (variations include Wihtlaeg, Withleig, Witlac, Huitlac, Huitlaic, Huitlaico). Uihtlag is Anglo-Saxon for "Odin's Law", indicating the he was embodiment of that Law. He made several treaties with the Emperor Theodosius I and eventually accepted an invitation in his last years to go to Constantinople and see the memorial to his father. Unfortunately a week of festivities proved too much for the elderly chieftain and he died there in 381. The Emperor gave him a magnificent funeral, which considerably impressed the Goths and others who saw it.

Vermund (Pharamond, Faramund, Warmund) succeeded his father in about 381. We do not know if he was present at his father's funeral and cannot know therefore whether there was an immediate take-over or not. Wenzler calls him a "legendary king" [7] and there is a story that he founded the Kingdom of the Franks in 425. However neither Gregory of Tours nor "Fredegar" agree with this statement and the Mercian Kings' List (a manuscript in the Royal Collection), record him as the son of Uihtlag. The Danish Royal Pedigree (Langfedgetal) calls him Vermund Vitre (The Wise) and shows him as an ancestor of Harald Hylthetan. Although this pedigree (Langfedgetal) dates only from the 14th century, it is almost certainly copied from an earlier possibly oral source.

Vermund's brother Ricimer (Richemer) was the Commander of Militia and Count of the Imperial Palace under the Emperor Gratian. Ricimer in turn had succeeded his elder brother Merobald (Mellobaud) in about 378. So powerful did Ricimer become that according to Oman, he "made and unmade emperors at his good pleasure for some twenty years."[8] Ricimer's son Teudemer had a daughter, who initially married a Cimbric king of Jutland and subsequently married Vermund's grandson Hlodio (Clodomir). I will be dealing with the question of the Cimbres a little later.

We now come to another interesting name. The Mercian pedigree gives the name of Vermund's son as Uffe or Offa and the Anglian poem *Wídsíö* calls Offa "The greatest of all mankind between the seas". This seems rather curious, as at first glance Uffe or Offa is otherwise little known. There was however a contemporaneous "Ulf" or Ata-Ulf, who was very well known. Uffe, Offa and Ulf are all variations of the same name. He was the Visigoth king, who together with Alaric, his brother-in-law, beat the Romans at Adrianople and later sacked Rome itself in 408 AD. Ata-Ulf means something like "The God Uffe or Ulf" or possibly "The ancestor Ulf". Uffe was the lineal descendent of Weoôulgeot and hence, King of the Visigoths. It would appear therefore that Uffe and Ataulf are one and the same. This is further confirmed by an Elchaisite genealogy, which we will encounter later on in this book, whereby Ata (-Ulf) married Maria "Of the seed of the blessed Elchasai".[9] He later married Galla Placidia, sister of the Roman Emperor, Honorius at Narbonne. Ataulf was killed in 415 AD and in 417 AD Galla Placidia remarried the Roman General Constantius, who then became Co-Emperor. I am not totally sure whether in fact Maria had died or if Ataulf, like many of the kings at the time, was polygamous. Certainly Galla "divorced" her husband Constantius to marry Ataulf and when Ataulf was killed, promptly remarried Constantius.

Vermund also had two daughters, the first of whom married Alaric, King of the Visigoths, and who died in Italy in 409[10] and the second of whom married Vallia. Ataulf succeeded his brother-in-law, Alaric, as King of the Visigoths and it was under him that they took over as kings of Rome. The Romans were naturally not very happy and an agreement was reached whereby Ataulf moved his people first to the area of Genoa, then on to Marseilles somewhere around 412 AD. It was there that he met and married Maria. From there theVisigoths moved to Aquitaine, after the death of Ataulf, who was actually killed in Barcelona. After a short while Ataulf was succeeded by Vallia, who became the founder of the Visigothic Kingdom of Toulouse and who died in Toulouse in 420. After Vallia, Theodoric I succeeded to the throne of the Visigoths. It is to be noted that Catalonia was originally Gotalonia. By 476 AD the Visigothic Kingdom extended from Nantes to Cadiz; in other words, the whole of Spain and southern Gaul. It remained that way until 507 AD, when the Visigoths were defeated by the Franks at Vouillé. Their Spanish Kingdom remained until overrun by the Moors in 711 AD.

At this point I am going to deal quickly with the Cimbres. Cimbre and Cambri are a shortened form of Sicamber, which was the old name for the Franks. At the baptism of Hlodovech, King of the Franks,

Gregory of Tours quotes Bishop Remigius as saying, "Meekly bow thy proud head, Sicamber".

One of the major problems when dealing in early genealogies that have been Latinised is the use of the word "Filius". Normally one would translate this as "Son", but unfortunately it is used for both legitimate and illegitimate sons, adopted and step-sons and even for son-in-laws. It is also used sometimes to indicate descent from a particular person, for example "Davidi filius" means "son of David" but must be taken to mean descent from David. We have to bear this in mind when reading contemporary documents.

There is the beginning of a change to the line of Rhoes with the marriage of Ataulf to Maria of the line of Elchaisai. By the year 100 AD there was a considerable colony of Jews based around the semi-circle running from Marseilles through Narbonne to Toulouse, some of whom were of the Elchaisaic persuasion, a sort of early Judaic Christianity, which we shall be dealing with in a following chapter. From now on, from the line of Hlodio, a religious/law-giving authority starts to take shape. Previously the Odonic line had been composed of both War Chiefs and Pontiffs, but it seems that these two positions were now starting to split with Hlodio's line, becoming a type of priestly caste, whilst the line of Alaric takes on the war chieftain's role. Nonetheless, Hlodio's dominions extended from South Jutland, all the land between the Elbe and the Rhine and the whole of Thuringia, an inheritance from both his father and father-in-law. Often, however, the two positions were merged into one particularly strong person and he becomes more like the old Maccabean concept of a priest/king, who leads in time of war.

Hlodio (or Clodomir) was the son of Ataulf and Maria (of the seed of Elchaisai). Fredegar calls Hlodio the "son" of Teudemer, but as it is highly unlikely that Hlodio married his own sister, we may safely read "filius" to mean son-in-law. We know however that Teudemer's daughter (name unknown) had been married before to a Cimbric (Frankish) king, though there is a suggestion or implication here of rape. At all events she had a son by her previous liaison, whom she called Merovech, probably after his grand uncle Merobald. Merovech means son of Mero, in the same way that Brankovich means son of Branko and indicates descent from an eponymous. Merovech is also referred to as "Merovee the Older". From this line descends the Merovingian dynasty of France.

By her marriage to Hlodio, Teudemer's daughter, has at least two sons and a daughter of whom we can be sure. The eldest son is called Merovee and is often called Merovee the Younger. He was killed at the battle of Soisson. The next son of whom we have record is Hlodovech and there is a daughter (again, name unknown) who marries the son of Vallia's daughter and he is called Ricimer, after his great uncle. There seems to be a pattern in the family of calling sons after a great uncle.

The Romans, however, were extremely worried by this vast over-lordship on their doorstep, especially as it extended into areas governed by Rome. The Roman general Aëtius therefore adopted Merovech as his son and appointed him King of the Franks in the Low Countries and Northern Gaul.

Hlodovech or Chlodovehus[11] is left with the Burgundian part of his father's heritage, marries a Burgundian Princess, the only child of Gundahar, and adopts the Burgundian form of his name, Gundovech (or Gundobar or Gundiac). In 472 Ricimer dies, whereupon Gundobar takes control of the army of the Western Roman Empire, who are mostly made up of Franks, Burgundians and Visigoths anyway. Gundobar names Glycerinus as Emperor. This shows the power of these Gothic kings, but Julius Nepos marches on Rome at the instigation of the Eastern Emperor, Leo I.

Now follows a series of short term Emperors—Julius Nepos and Romulus Augustus—until the Roman Empire based on Rome is formally ended at Ravenna on 28th August, 476 AD. This is the high point of the Visigothic Empire, which extends from Gibraltar to the Loire Valley and from the Bay of Biscay to the Rhine Valley, with its capital in Toulouse.

In 496 AD Clovis I, now King of the Franks, led them to a victory over the Alemanni near to modern day Strasbourg. He later became a convert to Christianity and it is at his baptism that Bishop Remigius, or Remy, addresses him as "Sicamber". It is at this point that the Christian priests start to forbid the old King Lists showing descent from Odin, saying they are pagan myths, but as we shall see they had a more dark and ulterior motive.

In 502 AD Gundobar made clear his new position as lawgiver by issuing a legal code making Romans and Burgundians subject to the same law. However he was still the commander of what used to be the old Roman Army and, in 507 AD, allied himself with Clovis to defeat the Visigoths at Campus Vogladensis. Alaric II, now King of the Visigoths, was killed and Clovis annexed the Visigoth Kingdom of Toulouse.

However in 508, the Franks, in turn, were driven out of Provence by the Ostrogoths under Theodoric. The Ostrogoths also recovered Septimania (later called the Languedoc) from the Visigoths. The infant Visigoth heir, Amalaric, was Theodoric's grandson, so Theodoric stepped in and acted as Regent. Clovis meanwhile established his capital at Lutetia (now Paris).

The table on the following page shows the various lines of descent from Rhoes:

Ancient Gothic Kings

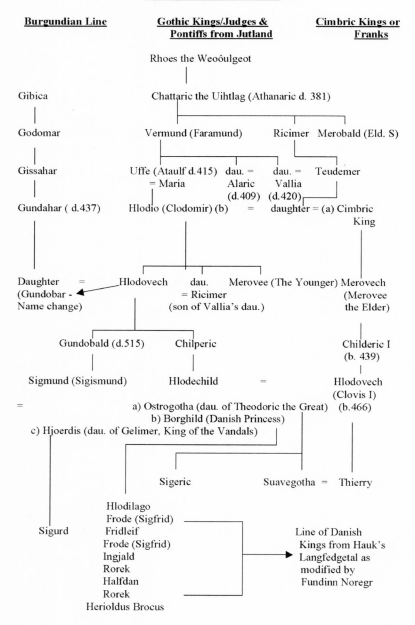

Burgundian Line

**Gothic Kings/Judges &
Pontiffs from Jutland**

**Cimbric Kings or
Franks**

Rhoes the Weoôulgeot

Gibica

Chattaric the Uihtlag (Athanaric d. 381)

Godomar

Vermund (Faramund)   Ricimer   Merobald (Eld. S)

Gissahar

Uffe (Ataulf d.415)   dau. =   dau. =   Teudemer
= Maria   Alaric   Vallia
(d.409) (d.420)

Gundahar (d.437)

Hlodio (Clodomir) (b)   =   daughter = (a) Cimbric
King

Daughter   =   Hlodovech   dau.   Merovee (The Younger) Merovech
(Gundobar -   = Ricimer   (Merovee
Name change)   (son of Vallia's dau.)   the Elder)

Gundobald (d.515)   Chilperic   Childeric I
(b. 439)

Sigmund (Sigismund)   Hlodechild   =   Hlodovech
(Clovis I)
=   (b.466)
a) Ostrogotha (dau. of Theodoric the Great)
b) Borghild (Danish Princess)
c) Hjoerdis (dau. of Gelimer, King of the Vandals)

Sigeric   Suavegotha = Thierry

Hlodilago
Frode (Sigfrid)
Sigurd   Fridleif   Line of Danish
Frode (Sigfrid)   Kings from Hauk's
Ingjald   Langfedgetal as
Rorek   modified by
Halfdan   Fundinn Noregr
Rorek
Herioldus Brocus

Gundobar's son, Gundobald, who confusingly is also often referred to as Gundobar, was also the great law-giver of his people. *The Lex Burgundionum* was his work. In Tit. III of this work he declares that Gundahar, his avus (his mother's father), was the son of Gissahar. Gregory of Tours (in Chap. 19) makes it quite clear however that his father, Gundioc or Gundobar, was descended from Athanaric. The genealogy, above, that I have drawn up shows that both these statements are possible.

According to the great Scandinavian Epic the *Edda*, Sigmund or Sigismund was a king in *"Frankland"*. "He married Borghild of Braalunda and stayed in Denmark in her realm." We know that Sigmund's first wife was Ostrogotha, the daughter of Theodoric the Great, and that she died after giving birth to a daughter. We also know that Sigmund married again and it is reasonable to suppose from the *Edda* that Borghild was his second wife.

The *Edda* goes on to say, "Thereafter he drew south to the kingdom he owned in Frankland and married Hjoerdis, daughter of King Oilime." We can work out, therefore, that he probably returned to his Burgundian/Low Countries territories about 515 AD, after the death of Borghild. King Oilime can be identified with Geilamir, King of the Vandals, dethroned by Belisarius in 534 AD. We also know that subsequent to Sigmund's death, Hjoerdis married Alf, the son of Chilperic (see table on previous page), whilst Chilperic's daughter, Hlodechild, married Clovis I.

The name Sigismund is interesting. It will be noticed that it is entirely different from all of his Odonic line forebears, but as we shall see later on, is derived from his Elchaisaic forefathers. It is one of the many little pieces of information that we shall be setting into our "jigsaw puzzle" as our story progresses.

Hlodilago, according to his own statement, was descended from Hlodio and claimed territory in the land of the Chatti as a consequence. His father Sigmund was a Woelfung and consequently descended from Ataulf; we can show therefore that the genealogical table that I have outlined previously is able to be cross-referenced with a number of different sources. This is important, as much of this work gives a somewhat different slant to the history that we have been brought up to believe.

The last bit of the genealogical table is, I'm afraid, restricted to one source — but that does not make it any less valid. It is certainly generally accepted in Denmark.

What this shows is that the Odonic Royal Families were closely related not only by family ties and marriages but also by religious customs and traditions. True, their economic and political interests sometimes diverged, which resulted in family feuds, and a considerable amount of bloodletting, but the idea of the Odonic bloodline was never forgotten. There is a document that purports to show the descent of the four main lines of the British Kingdoms from Odin, which was generally accepted until the coming of Christianity.

The descent for the Kingdom of Wessex is as follows:

```
                    Woden = Friga
                         |
                    Fredegar**
                         |
                      Frewin
                         |
                      Wigga
                         |
                     Grunisch
                         |
                       Esla
                         |
                      Elisius
                         |
     Cerdic the Saxon – King of Wessex
                         |
                      Keuric
                         |
                     Ceauliu
                         |
                      Cutha
                         |
                     Aelward
                         |
                     Keuried
                         |
                       Ina
                         |
                     Inigisil
                         |
                      Eoffa
                         |
                       Easa
                         |
                    Alkumund
                         |
                      Egbert
                    (802-839)
                         |
                   Aethelwulf
                         |
                Alfred the Great
                    (871-899)
```

** Some versions include Bældæg & Brond in between Fredegar and Woden.

The problem with the above genealogy is that even if we are generous and give 50 years between generations it only takes us back to 148 BC. Mostly one gives 30 years per generation, which would only take us back to 233 AD. However, let us not completely discard this genealogy just because it appears at first glance to be wrong.

If we suppose that in fact even 30 years is too much, and let's face it, life was short in those days, and that 23 years per generation is more like the mark, then it would take us back to Rhoes the Weoôulgeot (roughly 350 AD). We have already seen that Weoôulgeot means Chief of Odin-God. Let us suppose, therefore, that when this genealogy was written down many hundreds of years later, Weoôulgeot became shortened to Odin-God and then Woden. In fact, this may be simply another line from Rhoes.

During their migrations these families or tribes had come into contact with the classical pagan Roman and Greek civilisations and each had accommodated each other's particular beliefs and customs. It is probable that many of the Odonic beliefs were influenced and perhaps changed by the intercourse with these civilisations.

The problem came with the introduction of Christianity as the official and eventually only acceptable religion. The ethics, ideas and indeed arrogance of the Christian priests contrasted sharply with the idea of warfare and the warrior as being the ideal to strive for. Indeed, the Church had to invent the idea of the Christian knight to overcome this.

To some of the Odonic line, however, the ideas of Christianity were anathema and they found it impossible to steer a course that was acceptable to both. As a consequence, the friendship between Christians and the followers of the cult of Odin became impossible and the Nordic peoples eventually broke off relations with the rest of Europe, going their own way.

Once the Goths were driven out of Italy and Gaul became a Christian country at the end of the 6th century, the isolation of the Nordic peoples became complete for nearly two centuries. It was not until Charlemagne started crusades against the Nordic countries, followed by the hated priests, that the Odonic families awoke from their long slumber and counter-attacked with fearful Viking raids all along the coasts of Europe. These raids, as we shall see in a following chapter, were led by the descendents of the House of Brocus.

Chapter 1 References:

1. www.art.man.ac.uk/ARTHIST/Estates/Hamiltong.htm

2. Ibid.

3. Montgomery, B. G., (1968) – *Ancient Migrations and Royal Houses*, pp. 15-17, Mitre Press, London.

4. Ibid.

5. Daily Telegraph, 10th March, 2005.

6. Oman, Sir Charles, (1991 Edition) – *A History of the Art of War in the Middle Ages*, Vol. 1, Chap. II, Greenhill Books, London.

7. Wenzler, C. (1995) – *The Kings of France* p. 3, Editions Ouest-France, Rennes, France, Trans. Angela Moyon.

8. Oman, Sir Charles, *Op. Cit.*

9. See Appendix 2.

10. Zosima, *Historia*, Chap. 44 & 45.

11. *Liber Historiae Francorum*, Codex Petropolitanus, Ch. II.

Chapter 2

The Davidic and Elchasaic Lines

Many people assume that the Bible was written at or about the time that the events recorded in it took place, but this is far from the truth. The Old Testament does not predate in written form the return from Babylon. If one thinks about it logically it is highly unlikely that the Israelites taken captive to Babylon would have been allowed to carry with them any precious books, especially books in a language with which their captors were unfamiliar. It is probable that there were oral traditions and legends with which the slaves would have regaled each other during what free time they might have had, just as a later generation of slaves from Africa regaled each other during the twilight hours after their labours on the plantations.

The difference between the Israeli captives and the Africans was that whilst the African captives were by and large illiterate, amongst the Jewish slaves in Babylon there were some extremely literate and clever scribes. Many of these became scribes in the equivalent of the Babylonian Civil Service and would have learnt and read much of the religious legends of the Babylonian dynasty of the period, which in turn owed much to their predecessors, the Sumerians.

Either during the Babylonian captivity or immediately afterwards, these scribes set up an outline of the "People of Israel", putting into written form the legends of their people and, in the process, incorporating many Babylonian ideas whose form and content had been lacking in the Jewish religion up to that point.

Thus, for example, the story of the flood from Babylonian legend becomes a Jewish legend. Utnapishtim of Shurrapak/Fara, who in Sumerian myth built the Ark and saved the human race, becomes Noah in Jewish scripture.[1] The Code of Hammurabi, in turn becomes the Ten Commandments. One could go on almost *ad infinitem*, but I trust that two examples will suffice to prove my point. In fact, there have been numerous television programmes on just this subject, one recently called Secrets of the Old Testament, Channel 5 in the U.K., 5th April, 2005, showing how the work of archaeologists confirm the above.

Scholars generally divide the Old Testament into three or four groupings. These are known as the "E" documents, the "J" documents, the "EJ" documents and sometimes a fourth division is made with the "P" documents. The first three are so called because of the use of a particular word for "God" in Hebrew. In the "J" documents the Hebrew initials JHVH are used to indicate God, usually translated as Jahweh or Jehovah. In the "E" documents God is referred to either as Elohe or Elohim. Elohim is actually feminine plural, so should be translated "Goddesses", but the scribes of the post-Babylonian period were setting up an all male deity system. Therefore, in order to overcome this difficulty they announced that the "name of God was too holy to be uttered" and therefore, whenever a reader came upon any of these words they were to use the word "Adonai", Hebrew for Lord. Jews reading the Torah aloud still do the same today. So when you read "And the Lord spoke unto Moses" in English, you are perpetuating a priestly confidence trick, because it might say in the original "And the Goddesses spoke unto Moses", depending as to whether the word was Elohim or not. The last designation "P" is regarded as priestly interpolations in the original script.

"So," I hear you say, "the Old Testament wasn't written at the time of the events, but the New Testament was!" Well actually, NO! It is perfectly true that there were documents written at or just after the events recorded in the four Gospels, but they are not included in the Bible. They were declared at best, non-canonical, and at worst heretical. These include the Gospel of Thomas, The Gospel of Philip, the unexpurgated Gospels of Mark and Mathew, the Gospel of Mary (attributed to Mary Magdelene, but probably written by Mary of Bethany), the Gospel of Peter, the Gospel of the Essenes, the Gospel of Peace, the Gospel of the Egyptians, the Gospel of Truth and the Gospel of the Carpocratians, as well as the Apocrypha and the Acts of Thomas.

Some of these are well known to scholars, others are known only to a handful of specialists. For example, the best known is probably the Gospel according to Thomas. This starts with the words, "These are the words of the Secret. They were revealed by the Living Jesus. Didymus Judas Thomas wrote them down." Judah or Judas is his real name. Thomas comes from the Jewish word "Teum", meaning twin, and Didymus is Greek for twin. He was Jesus' twin brother and he is writing down the actual words of Jesus. (See Appendix 3.) This is the only Gospel which actually says this. Many of the stories and sayings of Jesus are identical with the other canonical Gospels, but with three major differences. In the Gospel of Thomas there is no "Virgin Birth", there are no miracles and there is no Resurrection. Instead there is resurrection during life, in the Gospel of Philip, in the form of a final initiatory rite. Jesus himself says, "Those who say that we first die and are then resurrected are wrong. Whoever is not resurrected before death knows nothing and will die." (See Appendix 3.) In Paul's second letter to Timothy (Chap. 1 v. 15), he admits that most of the Churches in Asia (by this he means what we would call the Middle East) no longer agree with him about the resurrection. He says Phygellus and Hermogenes deny the resurrection, but still consider themselves Christians. The Gospel of Thomas, the Gospel of Truth and the Gospel of the Egyptians form part of the Nag Hammadi collection and are some of the very earliest documents about that period. Scholars have now established that the very earliest forms of these scrolls date from no later than 150 AD, though the Nag Hammadi scrolls are copies made sometime before 400 AD.

I remember asking a Serbian Orthodox priest and scholar who attended one of my lectures in Zajecar, why the Gospel of Thomas was not canonical and I will always remember his answer. "It would only confuse the faithful." This is the trouble with all churchmen whether Catholic, Orthodox or other — they try to hide any document that might prove the contrary to the propaganda that they put out. They are in modern terms "Masters of Spin". The other documents which are known about are, apart from the ones mentioned in the previous paragraph, *The Jewish War* and *Antiquities of the Jews* by Josephus and the *Talmud*. All of these were written at or about the time of Jesus.

Generally speaking, the Gospels of Mathew, Mark, Luke and John were written any time between seventy to one hundred and fifty years after the events that they purport to record. Even the earliest was censored and changed by the early Pauline Church fathers after the Council of Nicaea in 325 AD. In view of the words of Thomas, it seems likely that the other four Gospel writers and their subsequent censors, the Church, used the Gospel of Thomas as the basis of their own writing, before going off into the realms of fantasy and fiction. We know, for instance, that Clement of Alexandria, one of the early Church Fathers who lived in the second century AD, writing to someone called Theodore, admits firstly to the existence of a secret or unexpurgated Gospel of Mark and what is more, says that other Gospels had also been doctored to cut out awkward bits. In his words, it is "better to lie" for the "good of the Church", than to tell the truth and admit the reality and bring the "Church into disrepute"[2].

There are, however, some fragments of documents that are known only to a handful of specialist scholars, amongst the foremost of whom is Yuri Stoyanov. Yuri was previously Yates Fellow at the Warburg Institute at the University of London and now divides his time, when not delving into archives in odd corners of the world, between the School of Oriental Studies, London and the University of Rome/Bologna, where he is Visiting Professor. He is also the author of the seminal work on the Bogomil/Cathars and the Hidden Tradition in Europe[3]. As the late Sir Steven Runciman wrote: "The author's knowledge of the relevant original sources is remarkable."

The first document we shall be looking at surfaced in the 16/17th century and appears to be a fragment from the unexpurgated Gospel of Mathew (Document 1, a few pages ahead). If one looks carefully at this document, which is in effect a genealogy, one will notice that it is in fact identical with the Gospel according to Mathew (I removed the "begats", and put it into computerised form). (See also Appendix 2.) St. Mathew (King James authorised version) starts with, "The book of the generation of Jesus Christ, the son of David, the son of Abraham." It then goes from Abraham to Joseph. Document 1 starts from Mathew v. 6 with David and continues to Joseph.

St. Mathew Chap. 1 v. 16 says, "And Jacob begat Joseph the husband of Mary, of whom Christ was born." At this point there is no suggestion that Jesus' conception is anything but normal. It is not until v. 18 that Mathew (or the Church) brings in the idea that Mary's son was not the son of her husband Joseph. If you read it carefully, even in English you can notice straight away that verses 18-25 have a different scan to the verses immediately preceding them.

In fact, v. 18 makes no sense. If this is "the generation of Jesus Christ, the son of David", then Jesus' claim to be of the Davidic Line comes according to Mathew himself, via Jesus's father Joseph. If Joseph is not his father then Jesus cannot be of the Line of David. You cannot have it both ways!

Document 1, however, goes somewhat further and calls Joseph "From Arimathea". This is curious as, according to the Church, Jesus' father was a carpenter but if we read Mathew a little more carefully, a different picture emerges. In Mathew chap. 27 v. 57-61 Joseph was a rich man from Arimathea, who was also Jesus' disciple. "He went to

Pilate and begged the body of Jesus. Then Pilate commanded the body to be delivered" (v. 58). "And when Joseph had taken the body, he wrapped it in a clean linen cloth" (v. 59). "And laid it in his own new tomb, which he had hewn out in the rock" (v. 60).

What is even more curious is that the only two people who could have asked for the body, under both Jewish and Roman Law, were either Jesus' son or his *father*. There is simply no getting away from this and, of course, Jesus would have been laid in the "Family" tomb. Again, if one looks at St. Mathew's Gospel closely, the husband of Mary—Joseph—appears at the beginning and then simply disappears. Joseph of Arimathea is never mentioned until Chap. 27, and then only as a disciple.

We are therefore left with very little alternative to the fact that the document appears to know more than the Church would have us believe. In other words, Joseph of Arimathea was Jesus' father—what is more, he is not a carpenter, but a "rich man". Is there any other confirmation of this? Well yes, there is! The Church Historian, Eusebius, writing at the beginning of the 4th century, but quoting Julius Africanus, who lived in the first century and knew Jesus' family, says that the "Master's family were taxed in Ramar". Now Arimathea is simply the Graeco-Roman name for Ramar or Ramatha, so we can conclude that the family were indeed from Arimathea.[4]

Document 1 goes on to say that Joseph married Miriam, which is what Mary would actually have been called in Hebrew, and that Joseph and Miriam had three sons——Jeshua (Jesus' real name), Jacob and Judah or Judas, again the real brothers of Jesus. But here the document makes further statements. It is quite clear that Jesus marries a lady by the name of Miriam, who is of the House of Bethany, of the house of Saul. This, of course, is particularly important, as his marriage to her would have brought back together the two kingly lines of Israel, those of the Benjamite line of Saul and that of the Davidic line.

The document then says that they had a daughter and that her name was possibly Mary (or again Miriam). However, there is a further liaison or possibly marriage with another Mirium (note the change in spelling), this time Mary Magdelene, and that by her he has a son and possibly a daughter, called Sarah. This is of course precisely what the Cathars believed, according to the Catholic Church—that Jesus was actually the blood son of Joseph and Mary and that he married at least Mary Magdelene.[5]

At first sight one might dismiss this document out of hand and no doubt the priests of the various Christian persuasions will, but we have already shown that this document appears to know more than the Church, so let's examine matters further. In St. Mathew's Gospel Chap. 27 v. 60-61 it says, after Joseph has put Jesus's body in the tomb, "he rolled a great stone to the door of the sepulchre, and departed" (v. 60). "And there was Mary Magdelene, and the other Mary, sitting over against the sepulchre." (v. 61). Note the words "the other Mary". Evidently not his mother, for she is clearly referred to in v. 56 "and Mary the mother of James and Joses" (his brothers, whose real names in Hebrew would have been Jacob and Joses). Again, Chap. 28 v. 1 says, "came Mary Magdelene and the other Mary". So who is this other Mary? His wife? Well the Church could hardly allow the Gospel to say "And Mary his wife", could they! So it is becoming fairly clear that they have to pretend she is someone else — *The Other Mary*.

In fact, it would have been inconceivable that a Jewish man, who lived to be thirty-three years old, would not have been married in those days. It was an obligation and his parents would have automatically arranged his marriage to a suitable bride. Rabbinic teaching says that celibacy is "*Unnatural*". Indeed, no Jew could teach until he had married and fathered children.[6] It is only the Church's wilful refusal to accept the idea of the Saviour being married, except to the Church, that has obscured the obvious for so long.

Again, is there any other proof of Jesus' marriage? Yes, there is! The Gospel of Philip, when talking about the three Marys in his life, says they were "His Mother, his Sister and his *WIFE*." There is no doubt about this at all.[7] Is there any other confirmation that Jesus had children? Again, there is. Eusebius, again quoting Julius Africanus, talks of the Desposyni and calls them "The descendents of the Master" and what is more, that they kept genealogies showing their aristocratic descent. (See note 4 and Appendix 5.)

Document 1 also suggests that Mary Magdelene was perhaps not a wife, but a concubine or mistress. Is there any other document that suggests this? Again, the Gospel of Philip says, "There were three who always walked with the Lord: Mary, his mother; the sister of his mother; and Miriam of Magdala, known as his companion (koinonos)." The word for copulation or mating in Coptic is "koinonia", and "koinonos" clearly indicates a sexual partner. But then, why does the next line talk of Mary his wife? Are they perhaps not the same person? Is Mary his wife and Mary of Magdala his concubine? It is at least a possible reading of this paragraph and appears to back up Document 1. (See note 7.)

The next point to consider is why these two women were "sitting over against the sepulchre". Obviously they were "Sitting Shiva" (The Jewish Family formal mourning). Again, the only people who sit "Shiva" are the immediate family. It follows, therefore, that both *Mary Magdelene* and the *other Mary* were immediate family. If they are neither mother nor daughter one must draw the conclusion that they are either both wives, or wife and concubine. Before everyone goes off the deep end please remember that having more than one wife was perfectly legal for a Jew of that period, especially if you were a "Royal" — Herod being a good example. However, as it is probable that Jesus' parents arranged his first marriage, with which no doubt he would have gone along as a dutiful son, it is possible that the second liaison was one chosen by himself. We shall examine this in more detail later on. Interestingly, the Montanists, an early Judaic Christian sect, specifically came out against having two wives, which suggests that the practice was commonplace.

The document also says that Mary Magdelene is of the "House of Æthiopia". Let us be careful about the word "Æthiopia". It has nothing to do with the modern country of Ethiopia, but is simply Greek (the language that much of the people of the region would have spoken and probably the original language of St. Mathew's Gospel) for "The land of the burnt-face people" and was used for any dark-skinned person, but particularly for the Arabian Semites or Nabateans (or Sabateans), whose territory surrounded the Tetrachy of Herod, with their Capital in Petra. Historically, the Bible called them the Edomites. Recent archaeological discoveries, however, prove that the Sabatean or Sabaean civilisation lasted for some 14 centuries from around 800 BC to 600 AD and included most of modern Ethiopia as well as southern Arabia.[8]

Prof. Morton Smith discovered a secret but expanded version of the Gospel of St. Mark, which he believed originated in Egypt[9] and points out that Mathew's Gospel was also known to exist in an expanded form, that originated in Syria.[10] It seems likely, therefore, that the document was part of the original and expanded version of St. Mathew's Gospel, which the Church deleted from the final "approved" version for obvious reasons. (See Appendix 2.)

Document 1

(Called the House of David)

King David of Israel
(begat on the wife of Uriah the Hittite)
Solomon
Roboam
Abia
Asa
Josaphat
Joram
Ozias
Joatham
Achaz
Ezechias
Manasses
Amon
Josias
Jechonias
Salathiel
Zorobabel
Abiud
Eliakim
Azor
Sadoc
Achim
Eliud
Eleazar
Mathan
Jacob = Tirah
|
Joseph (From Arimathea) = Miriam
|

| Jeshua | Jacob | Judah |

= (a) Miriam (of Bethany of the House of Saul)
|
A daughter (*Fragment missing*) (*Mary?**)*

≈ (b) Mirium (of the House of Æthiopia known as [*Fragment missing*] Magdelene)
|
A son (*Fragment missing*) (*& possibly a daughter Sarah?*)**

** The names in these brackets have been added by me as being the most likely choice.

The computerised format is mine. I left out all the other "begats". This was originally published in *Montgomery Millennium*.[11]

Let us consider this document for a moment. Let us suppose that the author, living in the 17th century, translates this document and realises what he has. What could he do with it? To publish it would have been unthinkable. You could go to prison—or worse— for heresy. So it becomes a secret, hidden document to be shown only to a few family members. Even today the Established Church steadfastly denies that Jesus was married and had a family.

The next document that we are going to consider, Document 2, is again a type of genealogy. This is again one of the documents which we shall be looking at that formed part of the collection believed translated by the same person.[12]

It will be noticed immediately that this document starts where the other apparently finishes, but appears to be produced from a female perspective. The main person here is Mary, not Jeshua. It is the daughter who is important, her husband's name seems almost an afterthought. Again, Mary's daughter Ruth is important; we do not even have a name for the son. Throughout this genealogy it is the female line that seems to be important until Maria. We will return to this point in a later chapter. For the moment, readers should pay special attention to the comments. As stated earlier, this book is a jigsaw puzzle.

This document is, I believe, Cathar in origin. Previously, I had thought this was possibly a fragment of the Book of Elchasai[13] or more correctly, the Book of Love of the Holy Elchasai, but I now think this was produced by a Cathar Family whom claimed descent from Elchasai. We may even have been able to identify who this family was. So who was Elchasai? Most of the information that we have about the Elchasaites comes from the work of one of their disciples, Mani, who is probably better known than the Elchasaites themselves, for the so-called "Manichaean" heresy named after him. In 1988 a Greek document was discovered and translated into German and published as *Cologne Mani Codex*[14], which gives considerable information about the Elchasaites. Here I am going to give only those parts that I consider relevant, much of which comes from Yuri Stoyanov's work.[15]

The Elchasaites were an early Judaic-Christian sect who were also called *Mughtasilab* (which means short-cut, because they had a short-cut to God) by al-Nadim and *Katharioi* (from which we get the name Cathar) in the Manicheaen work, *Kephalaia*. They were named after their founder, Elchasai (which means "Hidden Power") and who was active in the early second century. According to their tradition, Elchasai possessed a book, later called the "Book of Elchasai", which had been revealed to him by an Angel of Enormous size, called The Son of God. (The Book of Mormon was supposed to have been revealed by an Angel, as was the Koran). However, in the case of Elchasai, the enormous Male Angel was accompanied by an equally large Female Angel, called The Holy Spirit.[16]

Elchasaites believed very much in ablutions. The sound of running water was holy to them. With some exceptions they kept the Jewish Law, the Law of Moses. They regarded Jesus as simply another prophet in a long line of Jewish prophets, but Elchasai and his descendents were regarded as a continuous prophetic line. Actually their belief structure was quite complicated, with a belief in a Good God and an Evil God and very much dualistic in nature. It was also dualistic in the sense of male and female. Within a century after Elchasai's death there were sects in Rome, Palestine and Syria (from where the expanded version of Mathew is supposed to have come) and they were said to worship two Goddesses of the "Seed of Elchasai", Marthous and Marthana.[17]

The Babylonian Elchasaites, to which group Mani and he father belonged, did not eat meat or drink wine and carried out frequent fasting and purifications of both their food and their bodies by ritual ablutions with water.

Importantly for us, they are supposed to have had a secret book and their own Gospel, written at the time of Jesus in which they identified a cyclical reincarnation of a Messianic Christ. Elchasai was supposed to be the latest incarnation. Intriguingly, a previous incarnation was Buddha.[18] They totally rejected Pauline Christianity, which they called "The Way of the Greeks". They were, in effect, one of the first Judaic-Christian Gnostics and were to be the forerunners of the great Gnostic movement in Europe, which became the Cathars and Bogomils, and which probably owed much to the Essenes.

Document 2

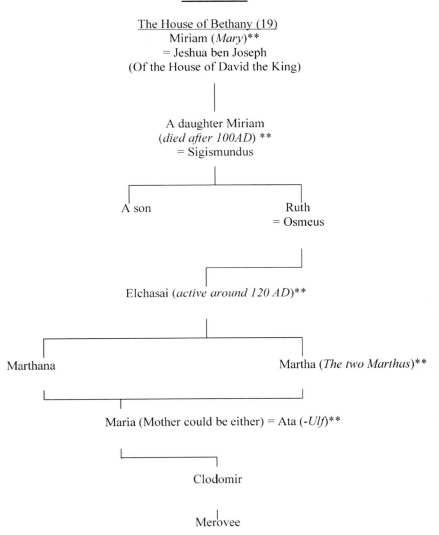

The House of Bethany (19)
Miriam (*Mary*)**
= Jeshua ben Joseph
(Of the House of David the King)

A daughter Miriam
(*died after 100AD*) **
= Sigismundus

A son   Ruth
                                      = Osmeus

Elchasai (*active around 120 AD*)**

Marthana   Martha (*The two Marthas*)**

Maria (Mother could be either) = Ata (-*Ulf*)**

Clodomir

Merovee

** The comments in these brackets are mine

The first thing that becomes obvious is that this document agrees to a certain extent with the first, but without mentioning Mary Magdelene. The first part down to Ruth is confirmed by Barbara Thiering's researches.[20] There are, however, a number of problems and apparent inconsistencies, not only with known facts, but also with the genealogy of the Ancient Gothic Kings given in Chapter 1.

According to Barbara Thiering, the daughter of Jesus and Mary of Bethany was born circa AD 30 and her daughter Ruth, circa AD 60. This would put Elchasai's birth around circa AD 80 and therefore put his ministry beginning in circa AD 120.

The problem was that between Elchasai's birth and his supposed grandaughter Maria's marriage to Ataulf in c. 412 AD, there was a matter of some 300 years. In other words, there were missed generations. Equally, the Gospel of Mathew does not have enough generations. It looked, therefore, as if these genealogies had been written down some years after the events by people who had lost the originals and were working from memory.

I sent an urgent e-mail to Yuri to ask for his help and wondered if Elchasai was a title rather than a name. He promised to check sources and come back to me. As it happened, he was in London over Christmas, 2003 and came to stay with my wife and myself between Christmas and New Year's. During those 24 hours we had a real brainstorming session and we were able to exchange the fruits of our individual researches. One of the bits of research from Yuri was that there had been several Elchasais and that there had been one at the time of Jesus. This was good news from my point of view. It was obvious that where the document stated Elchasai, it did not mean a particular person, but a succession of office bearers. The question was, were these successors in office related? Did the succession go from father to son?

If the name of the office was "Hidden Power", it suggested that the holder was a secret leader. So who would he have been at the time of Jesus? The Elchasaites regarded Jesus as a prophet, so he was an obvious candidate for the title "Hidden Power". But the Elchasaites were also heavily into purification by water, *a la* John the Baptist. He was therefore also a possible candidate. It occurred to me that Joseph of Arimathea, said to have started the Church in Glastonbury, was also a contender. There was another intriguing thought. The genealogy appeared to give prominence to females. Was it possible that Elchasai could be a female? After all, by 300 AD the sects in Rome and Palestine were said to be worshipping the two "Goddesses", Marthous and Marthana (in the genealogy, Marthana and Martha). This was a bit of a jigsaw puzzle in its own right.

I decided to start with John the Baptist and look at his claim to be Elchasai. The first thing to be noticed is that the Gospel stories of John the Baptist and the stories of the Johanite Christians or the Mandeans do not agree on a number of important points. In St. Mathew's Gospel, the story of John starts somewhat baldly. Chap. 3 starts, "In those days came John the Baptist, preaching in the wilderness of Judea, and saying Repent ye: for the kingdom of heaven is at hand. For this is he that was spoken of by the prophet Esaias, saying, the voice of one crying in the wilderness, prepare ye the way of the Lord, make his paths straight." (v. 1-3)

John was preaching an apocalyptic vision. The Jewish people expected deliverance from the Roman oppressors. They expected a Messiah, who would come to free them. They expected all the world's people to accept the God of Israel and the End of the World. The word used for Lord clearly defines that Lord refers to *God*, not to some earthly person, so there is no chance that it refers to John making the paths straight for Jesus. The same wording is used in St. Mark's Gospel, Chap. I v.3. The same words occur in the Dead Sea Scrolls and again in Luke, Chap. 3 v. 4. But only in Luke do you get the story of John being the son of Zacharias and Elizabeth. However, according to Lady Drower, the Mandeans have a similar story but with some differences. It is Elizabeth who declaims, "My Soul doth Magnify the Lord" and, according to the Mandeans, the *Magnificat* has been stolen from the story of John and appropriated by the early Christian Church for Mary.[21] In fact, another early Church father, Irenaeus, writing in 170 AD, admits that these words were spoken by Elizabeth and not Mary.[22]

The Mandeans regard John as *The Messiah* and maintain that Jesus usurped his position. From the Mandeans, too, one learns the name of John's wife, Anya. There are several, what one might term love poems, addressed by John to Anya, of whom he was obviously very fond. Yet if you read the Gospels you would think John was some sort of "Ascetic", living wild, as found in Matthew, Chap 3 v. 4, where it states he ate locusts and wild honey and had a raiment of camel's hair. Wild locusts in honey, by the way, were a Middle Eastern delicacy. They still are. Today, *Camel Hair Coats* are prized possessions of the Arabs, used to keep them warm in the cold desert nights. No doubt they were then. So John was not some wild, ascetic celibate monk, but a man with a home, wife and children, who was able to afford a Camel Hair Coat and dine on Middle Eastern delicacies.

The Mandeans, too, go in for ablutions near running water, just like the Elchasaites. John of course is most famous for baptising, but his disciples also fasted and abstained from wine. St. Luke's Gospel goes on to say that Zacharias was a priest of the course of Abia (one of the priestly Orders, which were generally inherited). It goes on to say that Elizabeth was of the "Daughters of Aaron", the most important of the priestly families. Any child of theirs therefore could well have held the title *Elchasai*. However, priests of the Order of Abia did not just come from Jerusalem. They might also come from the great Jewish Temple in Egypt, or indeed from the Nabatean/Sabatean Capital, Petra (now in modern Jordan).[23]

However, I was also looking for a family link to the later Elchasais, which appeared to come via Joseph or Mary. Was there a family link? According to Luke Chap. I v. 36, Mary and Elizabeth were cousins. A family link therefore had been tentatively shown, but I am very suspicious of links that only come from Church sources. There was, however, another difference with the Mandean Story. The Mandeans maintained that John was several years older than Jesus and not a few months, as is suggested by Luke's gospel. Indeed, if you read Mathew and Mark, one would also suppose that John was the older by many years. This is confirmed indirectly by Irenaeus. There was even a John Gospel in which John is the Messiah and not Jesus. In this version John's mother, Elizabeth, flees with her infant son into the hills. Herod sends his men to question John's father, Zacharias, who maintains he does not know where his wife and son are. Herod's men come back to tell Herod. "Herod was wroth and said: His son [Zacharias' son] is to be king over Israel."[24] It was fairly obvious that there existed a body of literature about John that predated the Jesus Gospel stories and in which John was the Messiah of a priestly and kingly line. For the time being I left the position of John as it was, and went on to look at Jesus being "Elchasai".

His candidature was fairly obvious. He was shown as the ancestor of Elchasai in the genealogy. He was certainly a "Power" in some circles. He led a rebellion against the Romans, which was unsuccessful, from a Jewish point of view, if they were looking for an "Apocalyptic Messiah". His position as a descendent of the House of David, married to a descendent of the House of Saul, would indeed have made him a hidden power. But although he was baptised himself by John, he was not a "Baptiser", per se. He certainly had people who worked around running water and we know he sailed on water, but water seemed to play a very small part in his rituals. One must, however, be careful on this point and remember the ever-present Church censorship. They may have omitted baptising from his reported works, so as not to look as if he were copying John.

There is, however, a very considerable body of opinion which maintains that Jesus was John's disciple to start with, and that John chose him somewhat against his (John's) will to take over and lead his group after him. John is supposed to have sent his disciples to Jesus to ask Jesus if he was the one that should come, or should they look for another, but it could also be read as, "Are you willing to come after me (e.g. Take over as head of my group) or do I look for another?" In this case, there is a rather different slant on the usually accepted dogma.

Along these lines there is an additional, intriguing thought. When Jesus is baptised by John, according to Luke Chap. 3 v. 22, the Holy Spirit descends in the form of a dove. Jesus is also referred to as "The Son of God". The Elchasaite's Holy Book is supposed to have been given to them by two Angels called "The Son of God" and "The Holy Spirit". Was there some connection? Was this a reference perhaps to Jesus receiving "The Book" or "The Word" from John?

In another contemporaneous document, "The Gospel of Peter", Jesus' cry on the cross is translated as, "My power, my power, you have left me."[25] Was he announcing that he was giving up that power to someone else? The words given in St. Mark's Gospel are "Eloi, Eloi Lama Sabachthani" and in St. Mathew's as, "Eli, Eli Lama Sabachthani". Yet nobody seems to understand these words; they suggest he is calling for Elias.[26]

El-cha-sai means Hidden Power. It seems that the reason nobody, Jews included, understood what he said is that these were "Hidden Words" to his successor. Effectively, he is saying, "Take over as Elchasai!"

To whom did he say this? We know, according to St. Mathew, that there were a number of women watching including Mary Magdelene and Mary, the mother of Joses and James. Immediately afterwards there is a reference to Joseph of Arimathea as if he, too, had been watching. This is confirmed in Mark. In St. Luke, however, Chap. 23, v. 46, Jesus says, "Father, into thy hands I commend my spirit" and gives up the ghost. Now, presumably, he actually said the words given in Mathew and Mark, as well as the words in Luke. What is more, everyone there seems to understand the words. In John the whole episode of the words are omitted.

Now almost everyone assumes that *Father* means *God,* on the basis that God was Jesus' father, but does it? What if Jesus is actually appointing his father, Joseph of Arimathea, to take over as *Elchasai,* witnessed by the other members of the group?

Carpocrates (according to Irenaeus) believed that Jesus was the son of Joseph and was brought up in Judaism, then turned to a higher truth and received a supernatural or hidden power,[27] possibly after a trip to India.

There is even a further bit of intriguing information. There is a considerable body of tradition stating that Joseph of Arimathea accompanied the two Marys and a Barnabas as far as Italy, near to where Lucca is today. There they are supposed to have parted, after some sort of an argument, and that Joseph went on to Britain. Did the women want one of their sons to become Elchasai? This is, I admit, pure speculation, but it is interesting none the less.

For the time being, my tentative hypothesis is that John had been "Elchasai" and had handed his position to Jesus, who in turn had handed it over to Joseph, pro tempore. We shall return to this at a later stage in the book.

The next point to consider is, who had been the Elchasai after about 200 AD? When I first considered this, I thought that perhaps Mani had been Elchasai and that he had been thrown out by the cult's hierarchy when he tried to bring together the different strands of Judaism, Christianity and Zoroastrianism. I now think that although this remains a possibility, it seems unlikely unless he married into the family, and there seems no confirmation of this in any Manichean work.

We know that by about 250 AD, the female descendents of the last known Elchasai were being worshipped as twin Goddesses. From the above information it is possible to work out the missing generations approximately, and they come out as follows:

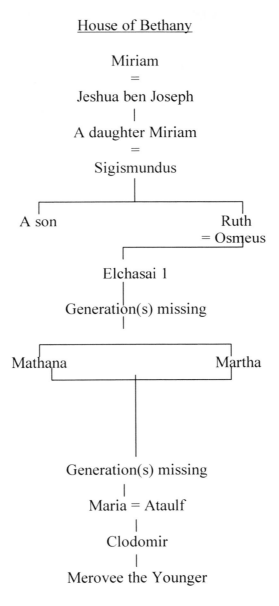

House of Bethany

Miriam
=
Jeshua ben Joseph
|
A daughter Miriam
=
Sigismundus

A son   Ruth
= Osmeus

Elchasai 1

Generation(s) missing

Mathana   Martha

Generation(s) missing

Maria = Ataulf
|
Clodomir
|
Merovee the Younger

From this information we can now give a date for this document in its original form, which is about 428-430 AD. We can also surmise that it was probably produced by or on the orders of Clodomir. We can say this with some authority, as Merovee the Younger was born circa 428.

There is no mention of his brother Hlodovech, who was born about 430 AD and we know that Clodomir's eldest son, Merovee the Younger, was killed at the siege of Soisson.[28]

Chapter 2 References:

All quotes from the Bible come from King James (Authorised) Version (1970), British and Foreign Bible Society, London.

1. www.art.man.ac.uk/ARTHIST/Estates/Hamiltong.htm

2. Smith, M. (1974) – *The Secret Gospel*, p. 70, Victor Gollancz, London. For the comments on the Epistle to Timothy see p. 127 and Second Epistle toTimothy, Chap. 1. v. 15. See also Appendix 3.

3. Stoyanov, Y. (1994) – *The Hidden Tradition in Europe*, Penguin Books, London.

4. Eusebius 3:19 (Eusebius – *History of the Church from Christ to Constantine*, translated by G. A. Williamson, Harmondsworth 1981). See also Catholic Encyclopedia, Ramatha and/or Ramleh; also Appendix 5.

5. Ibid., pp. 222-223.

6. Schneid, H. (1973) – *Marriage*, p. 4, Keter Books, Jerusalem, Israel. Also Ben Schorim, S. (1978) – *Mon frère Jésus*, Editions du Seuil, Paris. Also Abecassis, A. & Eisenberg, J. (1978) – *A Bible ouverte*, vol. 1, p. 125, Albin Michel, Paris.

7. Leloup, Jean-Yves (Translator) – (2003) – *The Gospel of Philip*, p. 65, Inner Traditions, Vermont, USA.

8. Edomite - http://www.ancientroute.com/empire/edom.htm 08/08/2005. Sabatean – http://cc.msncache.com/cache.aspx?q=276147039120&lang=en-GB&mkt=en-GB& 28/12/2005.

9. Smith, M. (1974) – *op. cit.* p. 142, Victor Gollancz, London.

10. Ibid.

11. Montgomery, H. (2002) – *The Montgomery Millennium*, App. III –8, Megatrend, Belgrade & London, but see Appendix 2.

12. Yuri Stoyanov is of the opinion that they were all translated by the same person and I see no reason to doubt his opinion.

13. Stoyanov, *op. cit.* p. 272-273.

14. Ibid., pp. 87-88.

15. Ibid.

16. Ibid.

17. Ibid., also see Szekely E.B. (1996) – *The Gospel of the Essenes*, p. 126, C.W. Daniel & Co. Saffron Walden, UK, in which he points out that the Dead Sea Scrolls show influences of the sacred books of the Avestas (India).

18. Ibid.

19. Montgomery, op. cit. p. III-7 – Collection Cornelius Hamsfort (1546-1627).

20. Thiering, B. (1992) – *Jesus The Man*, Chronology, BCA, London.

21. Drower, Lady E.S. (1937) – *The Mandeans of Iraq & Iran*, Oxford Univ. Press.

22. Kraeling, C. H. (1951) – *John the Baptist*, p. 169-170, Scribner's Sons, London. See Also James M. R. (ed.) (1953) – *The Apocryphal New Testament*, Clarendon Press, Oxford.

23. It must be remembered that Jerusalem was not the only Jewish Temple. In fact, the Temple in Egypt was at least as important, if not more so. Many priests went to Egypt to be trained and Joseph and Mary, with the infant Jesus, are supposed to have taken refuge there. See also Smith, M. *op. cit.* p. 82.

24. Kraeling, C. H. (1951) – *John the Baptist*, Scribner's Sons, London. See also Drower, Lady E.S. (1937) – *The Mandeans of Iraq & Iran*, Oxford Univ. Press.

25. Smith, M. *op. cit.* p. 104, quoting the Gospel of Peter.

26. St. Mathew Chap. 27, v. 47 (KJV).

27. Smith, M. *op. cit.* p. 134.

28. de Montgomery, B. G. (1968) – *Ancient Migrations and Royal Houses*, p. 118, Mitre Press, London – quoting French Chronicles.

Chapter 3

Jesus and his Family

Before proceeding any further with our jigsaw puzzle, it is advisable to go through what is known about Jesus as a person—his life, his friends and family.

One of the things about the Canonical Gospels is that he goes from being a baby in swaddling clothes to an adult. There is no story of his childhood. There is nothing about him playing with other children, running around as all children do, falling over and scraping his knees or hands. There is nothing about his youth. We know he was circumcised. We know he was brought up as a Jew. He must have studied the Torah—all Jewish children had to, but where? Did he study in Jerusalem or at home, or did he perhaps go to Egypt to study at the priestly school there? His cousin John studied there, according to the Mandeans, and it seems likely, therefore, that he did, too. We need, however, to be careful as to whether Egypt meant the actual country or the Qumran "Egypt".[1]

We also know that he had brothers—James (or Jacob), Joses, Simon and Judah or Judas (also called Thomas),[2] and possibly others. The brothers Simon-Peter and Jacob were crucified in Jerusalem on the orders of Tiberius Alexander (Procurator for Rome, 46-47 AD), though there is some doubt as to their death. We know, too, that he had one or more sisters, one of whom was called Salome.[3] It is likely that she was the source, if not the writer, of the Gospel of the Carpocratians (or Gospel of Salome).[4] This is all quite a normal Jewish family for the time—or indeed for the present. Life in Israel has not changed in many ways. Morton Smith says that St. Mark's Gospel originally included a conversation between Salome and Jesus, but that it was deleted. He goes on to say that in early Christian literature Salome was a very shady lady, but nobody seems to know why![5] Document 1 does not mention either Joses (Joseph) or Simon, but St. Mathew does. It is possible, therefore, that both Joses and Simon are half-brothers or were born after Document 1 was originally written. However, as Document 1 mentions Jesus' children, presumably Joses and Simon would be alive. I think it likely, therefore, that they were half-brothers. (See subsequent chapter.)

The other person who appears of great importance is Mary Magdelene, considering the Church's antipathy to the idea that Jesus could have girl friends. It is assumed that she is called Magdelene because she came from Magdala, which, so far as I am aware, is only mentioned once and then only in one Gospel as the "Coasts of Magdala".[6] Interestingly, there is a Magdala in modern Ethiopia. She obviously followed Jesus around, but equally was not the only woman in his life. In Mark Chap. 8 v. 2 & 3, Mary is only one of several women including "Joanna, Susanna and many others, which ministered unto him of their substance."[7] In other words, they paid his bills!

The most important person, however, according to Documents 1 and 2, was Mary of Bethany, his wife. She is almost completely ignored in the official Gospels. This is hardly surprising, as the Church took pains to pretend that Jesus was a celibate ascetic—though it hardly accords with his being accused of sitting down with sinners and publicans and being a "wine-bibber". What do we know about her from the Gospels? She is mentioned in St. John's Gospel as being the sister of Martha and Lazarus of Bethany.[8] She is mentioned again with her sister Martha in St. Luke's Gospel.[9] Although the Church has cut out all reference to her as wife, there are nonetheless hints in the Gospels to that effect. For example, Jesus is in the house of Mary's brother, Lazarus, in Bethany when a woman with an alabaster jar anoints his head with costly perfume.[10]   Now that was a common custom in Egypt. You can see it on many murals, with guests having perfume balls placed on their heads. It was frequently done by a young bride to her husband, particularly if you came from outside Judea itself. It was frowned upon by the more rigid Essenic Jews of Jerusalem, hence their disgust at this action. In particular, the word "head" may in fact mean phallus, as can be seen from the Egyptian Temple at Philae, the centre of the Egyptian/Jewish worship (see photo). In Luke Chap. 7 v. 37-8 a woman (not named) washed Jesus' feet with her tears and dried them with her hair, before anointing them with ointment. St. John's Gospel, Chap. 12 v. 3 specifically says this person was Mary, the sister of Martha and Lazarus, and that Jesus is in their house. In other words, this is Mary of Bethany, which both Documents 1 and 2 claim is his wife.

Annointing the Head (courtesy of D. Green)

This brings us to the next question. Where was Bethany? Bethany is mentioned in a few places in the official Gospels—in John, in Mathew and in Mark[12] and in two of those, Mathew and Mark, the ointment being placed on Jesus' head is mentioned. From reading these Gospels it appears that Bethany is somewhere not far from Jerusalem, but it is my opinion and Yuri Stoyanov concurs with me, that it was a place that became known as Bethany because people of a particular origin lived there. The people who lived there were from Bithynia, which is in Northwest Anatolia, next to the Sea of Marmora and the Black Sea. Helen, the mother of Constantine, was born there. It had been peopled mostly by Thracians, but the last kings had been little more than Roman puppets until, in 74 BC, their last king willed his country to Rome. Jews had been established there for more than 100 years. The people from that area, who had moved to Israel, were mostly of the rich merchant class, worldly and Hellenised, who took their Jewishness with a certain panache, but with none of the rigidity of the Pharisees. This would accord well with the fact of their supporting Jesus financially. Lastly, as we shall see in another chapter, it is not unlikely that they were descendents of the tribe of Benjamin or, at the very least, thought they were.

Is there any hint in the canonical Gospels that Jesus did marry? Again, it can be inferred from certain verses in John. Jesus is "called to the marriage" in Canae. His mother is clearly the hostess and it is implied that Jesus is the bridegroom. The governor of the feast "called the bridegroom" and complimented him on his new wine supply, but as it was supposedly Jesus who had supplied it, then it must follow that Jesus was the bridegroom.[12]

There is also another hint, again in St. John's Gospel. John the Baptist says, referring to Jesus, "He that hath the bride is the bridegroom: but the friend of the bridegroom (*John himself*), which standeth and heareth him, rejoiceth greatly."[13] This would suggest that John himself approved of Jesus' marriage.

To conclude, Jesus is born into a normal Jewish family—father Joseph, mother Mary, brothers Joses, Jacob, Judah and Simon and sister Salome. After a normal childhood he is sent to study in Egypt and probably to India. On his return he has an arranged marriage with a wealthy girl of Bithynian origin, called Miriam. They have a daughter called Miriam or possibly Salome, after his sister. He enjoys the company of women and has an affair or maybe a second marriage to another Mary. John, just before his death, makes him Elchasai. Jesus leads a rebellion against Rome and is defeated and crucified. Though, as we shall see in another chapter, there is some doubt that he died. His wife or widow has to flee Israel and eventually finds refuge amongst the Jewish colony near Marseilles where, incidentally, Herod had a villa.

According to the Encyclopaedia Britannica (p. 901), most modern scholars think that the character of Mary Magdelene is made up of three different Marys—Mary of Bethany, Mary the Penitent and Mary Magdelene herself. In Eastern tradition Mary Magdelene was the wife of St. John the Evangelist (or the Divine) and accompanied him to Ephesus, where she subsequently died. From the same source we learn that many scholars think both Mary the Penitent and Mary Magdelene anointed Jesus, one on his head and one on his feet.

From the dual line of Benjamin (Mary of Bethany) and David (Jesus), a new line of Elchasaite priest /kings evolved and married into the Odonic dynasty.

However, Document 1 makes it plain that Jesus had, at the very least, a liaison with Mary Magdelene and it is known that there used to be a document similar to Document 2, but which shows the descent from Mary Magdelene. Indeed, the Royal Family of Valois claimed descent from her. Regretfully, neither Yuri nor myself have been able to track this down.

There were still a number of unanswered questions. Who was Mary Magdelene? Why was John *Elchasai*? Why was John put into prison? Why did he decide to make Jesus his successor? I needed at the very least a working hypothesis!

The first starting point was a contemporary document—Josephus's *Antiquities of the Jews*. Josephus gives a very different reason for John's detention by Herod. According to Josephus, Herod was in the process of divorcing his wife, the daughter of King Aretas of Nabatea. In fact, the lady concerned found out about Herod's intention and fled to her father's capital of Petra. King Aretas was furious. He gathered together his army to invade Herod's territory, thoroughly trounced him and was only stopped by Roman threats from deposing Herod and taking over his Tetrachy. But why should this worry John?

Mentioned earlier was that John's father, Zacharias, could have been a priest from Nabatea. If his wife was "of the daughters of Aaron" then it was not unlikely that they were very high up in the Nabatean

Court, perhaps even related to King Aretas. There is little wonder then that John would have been furious and would have threatened Herod. It is also very likely that Herod feared an uprising from his own people led by John, who was very popular at the time. Alternately, Herod may have taken John captive as a hostage to bargain with, should King Aretas attack. Once the Romans had interfered and Herod felt safe, he could hardly let John go again to stir up trouble, so he had to execute him. The story in the Bible of Salome dancing for Herod and then requesting John's head on a charger was written years after the claimed event and is plain fiction.

However, Document 1 calls Mary Magdelene "of the House of Æthiopia". Was she, too, from Nabatea? Could she have been John's daughter? If she was, everything fits in nicely. John agrees to Jesus becoming his successor in return for him marrying John's daughter, Mary Magdelene. When John knows he is under sentence of death, he sends to Jesus, "Will you come after me (*and look after Mary*) or do I look for another?" Jesus agrees, and probably signs a *ketubbah*, a Jewish marriage contract[14], but his parents have already arranged a marriage for him to another Mary, from Bethany. It would dishonour the family if Jesus were to reject her. However, it is likely that John would have insisted on a *ketubbah* before giving his formal blessing. To all intents and purposes they would have been considered married, even if they were not co-habiting and frankly, it seems likely that they were. According to ancient custom, cohabitation could only take place after the bridegroom had delivered the *ketubbah* (wedding contract) to the bride and received the *nissu'in* (the marriage blessing). However, this could be done in front of witnesses, usually ten men.[15]

When John is condemned to death, Jesus, John's disciples (almost certainly including Mary Magdelene) and Jesus' own, all flee into the desert for a while. As they would have been considered by John's disciples to be married, it would have seemed strange had they not cohabited.

When Jesus returns, he has to marry Mary of Bethany for both family and political reasons, as we shall see later. However, polygamy was quite normal, particularly among the Davidic families. Curiously, it was the Hellenic non-Jewish converts who found the idea of Jesus' second marriage wrong.[16]

This hypothesis may seem at first sight unlikely, but as the fictional detective Sherlock Holmes famously said, "When you have eliminated the impossible, what remains, however unlikely, is the truth."

Chapter 3 References:

1. Thiering, B. *op. cit.* Chap. 10. According the Thiering there was a place-known as Egypt at Qumran.

2. Gospel according to St. Mathew (KJV), Chap. 13 v. 55. See also Document 1. See also Gospel of Thomas and Acts of Thomas—in both instances Judas is clearly labelled as his twin.

3. Gospel according to St. Mark (KJV), Chap. 6 v. 3; also Chap. 15 v. 40 & 41; also Chap. 16 v. 1. If Salome is the sister of James, Joses and Judah and they are Jesus' brothers, then presumably Salome is his sister.

4. Smith, M. *op. cit.* p. 70.

5. Ibid.

6. Gospel according to St. Mathew, Chap. 15 v. 39.

7. St. Mark (KJV).

8. Gospel according to St. John (KJV), Chap. 11 v. 1-5.

9. Gospel according to St. Luke (KJV), Chap. 10 v. 38-42.

10. St. Mark, Chap. 14 v. 3.

11. St. John, Chap. 11 v. 20, 28 & 29. St. Mark, Chap. 11 v. 1, 11, 12 & Chap. 14 v. 3. St. Mathew Chap. 26 v. 6.

12. St. John, Chap. 2 v. 9 & 10.

13. St. John, Chap. 3 v. 29. The Italics are mine.

14. The *ketubbah* had already been instituted by 100 BC. See Schneid, H. (1973) – *Marriage*, p. 24, Keter Books, Jerusalem.

15. Ibid.

16. Thiering, B. (1992) – *Jesus the Man*, p. 148, BCA, Gt. Britain. A section of the Damascus Document attacks the heretic (Jesus), "Caught in fornication...taking a second wife whilst the first is alive". CD4: 19-5:6.

Chapter 4

The Benjamite Line and its Betrayal
(This story is told in the Books of Samuel 1 & 2 and Judges)

If one reads the Bible cursorily, and most people do, one gains the impression that Saul was killed fighting the enemies of Israel and that David took over, acclaimed by all. However, if one reads the relevant parts of the Bible with care and compares them with the Haggadic and Talmudic traditions, a rather different picture emerges.

In order to understand the Benjamite tradition, it is necessary to start with the Prophet Samuel. If one reads Samuel Chapter 3, it is claimed that Samuel heard the voice of the Lord and God told Samuel all the things that he was going to do to Eli who, up until that point, had been the Chief Priest and, more importantly, "Judge" (effectively, Chief of his people—Rhoes was called Judge, as you may remember). If you happen to be like me and are rather sceptical about people hearing voices, or think that they need psychiatric help, then you might come to the conclusion that I came to. Namely, that Samuel wanted fast track promotion and when he did not get it, devised a rather nasty little game to get his way.

In fact, the whole episode may well have been written after the event in order to justify Samuel's actions against Eli and his sons. In Samuel 2:22 it states, "Now Eli was very old, and heard all that his sons did unto all Israel; and how they lay with women that assembled at the door of the tabernacle of the congregation." Samuel effectively does a take-over from an old man, who was good and kind, but whose sons, like all young men, needed some female company.[1]

Samuel eventually makes his bid for power. He is in Shiloh and arranges to have the two sons of Eli, Hophni and Phinehas, carry the Ark of the Covenant into battle in front of the Israeli army. When of course, as he expected, the Philistines overcame the Israelis, the sons of Eli were killed. When Eli hears that his sons have been killed and the Ark taken, he has a heart attack, falls down off the gate of the city and breaks his neck, or possibly commits suicide—one cannot be sure which.

Samuel is now in sole charge. You can read the whole story for yourself but it finishes with the words, "And Samuel judged Israel all the days of his life."[2] At least that is what he would have liked, but somehow what you sow, you reap. He tried now to make this Judgeship hereditary and appointed his sons as judges. The Israelis were not amused and decided that they would prefer a king.[3] Samuel did not take kindly to this idea at all. "But the thing displeased Samuel."[4]

Samuel tries desperately to persuade the people that a king is not a good idea. He has had supreme power for so long that he does not relish letting go. He tells them that a king will make their sons become charioteers and horsemen and runners and captains in the king's army. He will take the daughters to be cooks and bakers. He even says that a king will take the best fields and vineyards and give them to his servants (favourites). He goes on that the king will tax them a tenth on everything.[5] He goes on and on about how much better they would be by staying with him and not appointing a king, but to no avail. I suspect that he and his sons had been living the life of Riley at the people's expense for a very long time and that the people were fed up with them. "Nevertheless the people refused to obey the voice of Samuel; and they said, Nay; but we will have a king over us."[6]

Eventually Samuel has to give in. He pretends that he has prayed to the Lord and that God has heard their request and accepted his prayers. There had obviously been a great rally of protest by the people as Samuel eventually says that he will find them a king and they should all now go home.

Samuel now goes looking for someone who is not too bright, but is big and strong and will do what Samuel wants. Saul is not a well-educated person, but he stands head and shoulders above the average Israeli. He was also a Benjamite who were known as great warriors, but not of the educated class of scribes or priests. So Samuel anoints him, but tells Saul not to let on to anyone else. Samuel then tries a last chance to save his own power. He calls the people together at Mizpeh, and tells them that they have rejected God. "And ye have this day rejected your God...and ye have said to him, Nay, but set a king over us."[7] What he really means is, "How dare you reject me!"

Eventually he presents Saul to them as "Chosen by God". Not everyone is quite convinced,[8] but by and large people accept Saul. Samuel is, however, determined to hang on to power, even if Saul is king. So he writes in a book all the duties of the king,[9] which no doubt included a large amount of "Thou shalt obey Samuel in all things!" The people now go home, Saul gathers a small band of followers and goes home to Gibeah.

Shortly after this, Ammonites decided to try their luck against this new king. Saul proves himself a remarkably good general and proceeds to thrash the Ammonites. The Israelis now propose to put to death all those who spoke against Saul and demand that they come forward, but Samuel intervenes to save them, probably because he had been the instigator of the smear campaign and did not want them naming him. Naturally, he claimed that God had said so.

There is an interesting verse in Samuel, chapter 12, in which it is clear that Samuel is terrified that he may be sued for fraud (or the Biblical equivalent). "Whose Ox have I taken? Whose ass have I taken? Whom have I defrauded? Of whose hand have I received any bribe?"[10] He offers to make reparation. According to that same chapter, nobody takes him up on it... but one wonders. Politicians never change their ways.

As it happens, Saul is a pretty good king as kings go and Samuel becomes more and more marginalized. He is full of jealousy and envy of this young upstart who has, as he sees it, taken his power from him. He reminds me of Edward Heath sulking about Margaret Thatcher, taking what he saw as his rightful place.

Samuel reverts to type. He starts a nasty whispering campaign against Saul. All, of course, "In the name of the Lord". He demands that Saul slaughter perfectly good sheep and cattle as sacrifices, which of course were only eaten by the priests, and when Saul quite rightly refuses, says he has disobeyed God, and that God no longer wants Saul as king.[11] The Bible tries to pretend that Samuel leaves Saul in sorrow, but in reality I suspect that Saul effectively banished him.[12]

Samuel is now bent on revenge. He gathers together a small band of people who no doubt had benefited from Samuel's tenure of office and starts an underground rebellion. Eventually, he picks the youngest of Jesse's sons, David, to be his pawn.

Why the youngest? As any Jesuit will tell you—Give us the Child and we will gave you the Man. Much as the Bible tries to pretend that David was anointed by Samuel, before his run-in with Goliath, I personally think it unlikely. I believe that following David's popularity after the event, Samuel saw an opportunity to turn this to his own advantage. I think that he approached David at the time that David's head was full of the adulation of the crowds, when David felt he was the great conqueror. At the time that David was most vulnerable to this sort of talk, along comes Samuel and says, "After this great victory, don't you think you should be king?" David, probably drunk with success and not a little alcohol, replies drunkenly, "Of course!"

Later he regrets that he has been taken in by Samuel and tries to keep it all secret, particularly because Saul rewards him with money and offices and effectively takes David into his own family, by giving David his daughter, Michal. David therefore becomes Saul's son-in-law. Samuel, however, was not giving up. He persuades David to come to him in Ramah, Samuel's power base. The bit about Saul having an evil spirit and trying to kill David before he goes to see Samuel is a known priestly addition, a so-called "P" document.

What now happens, although the Bible tries to hide it, is civil war. Naturally, the enemies of Israel take advantage of the situation and attack. Saul has to fight them with only half his army. Initially he is successful and then turns his attention to dealing with David. In Samuel there follows chapter after chapter about the war between Saul and David, until the end of the first book of Samuel where Saul's forces, severely weakened by the civil war, fall to the Philistines. Both Saul and Jonathon are killed, together with two other of Saul's sons.[13] Samuel does not live to see the results of his perfidy, but dies sometime during the civil war.[14]

David now tries to take over the kingdom, but Saul's people and particularly his tribe, the Benjamites, continue to support Saul's line. They make Ishbaal (Man of Baal, later called Ishbosheth), king and defy David.[15] Chapter three of the 2nd Book of Samuel now makes it clear that the civil war continued for quite some time, but that eventually David won. "Now there was long war between the House of Saul and the House of David: but David waxed stronger and stronger, and the House of Saul waxed weaker and weaker."

So far I have been telling the story based purely on Biblical sources, though interpreting them for the modern reader. There is also Haggadic tradition—that when David eventually takes Jerusalem, he impales or crucifies all the remaining sons of Saul. But we now need to look at another document, which tells a somewhat different story about what happened to the tribe of Benjamin. But first we must look at a rather curious little story in chapters 19 and 20 of the Book of Judges. The story goes that a certain Levite, "when there was no king in Israel", took a concubine from Beth-lehem-judah. It goes on to say that this concubine played the whore and then returned to her father's house. Her husband (he is alternately called husband and master) goes to get her from her father and then journeys with her. On the way they stop at Gibeah, in the land of the Benjamites. Here they are invited to stay at the house of someone they meet and whilst they are eating, the men of the tribe of Benjamin come knocking on the door.

Judges 19 v. 22 takes up the story: "Bring forth the man that came into your house that we may know him." The owner of the house now makes a surprising offer to the Benjamites. "Behold, here is my daughter a maiden and his concubine; them I will bring you now...and do with them what seemeth good to you; but do not do so vile a thing."[16] It continues; " So the men took the concubine...and they knew her and abused her all the night until morning."[17]

In the morning her husband (master) finds her stretched out on the doorstep. Does he comfort her? No! He says, "Up, and let us be going."[18] When she can't get up on her own, he chucks her onto an ass and takes her home—and what does he do at home? He takes a knife and divides her body into twelve pieces. One hopes that she was dead beforehand. He now uses this as an excuse to inflame the rest of the tribes against the tribe of Benjamin. The remainder of the book of Judges is taken up with the civil war between the tribes of Israel and Benjamin and the fact that the Israelites slaughter not only the men, but particularly the women. In fact, according to chapter 21 all the women of the Benjamites were killed, so that they were forced to take wives from foreigners of Shiloh.

To me, this has always seemed an unbelievable story. First of all, it is supposed to have happened before the events in the book of Samuel. This is not likely, as not even Samuel would have been able to persuade the Israelites to accept Saul in the first place, after an event such as that just described. Secondly, one must appreciate that Samuel was himself one of the "Judges" and, in a sense, his Book One could have also been called "The Last Book of Judges".

We must therefore turn to our next document for enlightenment.

Document No. 3

"And it came to pass that a certain Levite took to wife a priestess of the Goddess (El/h/) and did dishonour her before the Goddess and whilst passing through the City of the Benjamites did tarry there. Now when the Benjamites heard of the dishonour done to the priestess they surrounded the house where the Levite was staying, but the woman did plead with them not to kill the Levite for he was also a priest. "Rather kill me for I am defiled."

And the Benjamites did as the woman asked and killed her and left her body by the door of the Levite.

And the Levite was exceeding wrath and did call upon the Tribes of Israel to rise up and smite their brothers the Benjamites and they did so for there was no King of Israel of the seed of Saul of the tribe of Benjamin.

And it came to pass that the Benjamites were mighty warriors and did smite the Tribes of Israel who numbered many. But after the third day the Tribes of Israel did by deceit enter into the City of the Benjamites and did kill the women and children. Then did the men of the tribe lose heart and were pursued even unto the hills.

And many passed out of the land of Israel and went to live in another place even unto Philistia and Arcassi and there they became mighty warriors for the men of Philistia and Arcassi worshipped the Goddess and they gave them their daughters to wives and the men of Benjamin dwelt there."[19]

******

There are a number of interesting things to note here. The first is that the Benjamites are clearly stated to be worshippers of the Goddess and not of Jahweh. The city of the Benjamites referred to in the third paragraph is almost certainly Jerusalem, which was at that time part of the Benjamite inheritance. David needed to occupy Jerusalem to establish his own undisputed reign. If one reads the book of Judges carefully one will find continuous references to some of the Israelites turning to worship other Gods and Goddesses. "And there arose another generation, which knew not the Lord."[20] "And they forsook the Lord and served Baal and Ashtaroth."[21] It seems that the judges/priests had considerable difficulty in persuading some if not all of the Israelites to worship this one God of theirs. Also note from Chapter 2 that even in the Bible (in those parts known as the "E" documents), there is reference to the feminine plural "Elohim".

The second thing to notice is that it is the Levite who dishonours the priestess, who in the Biblical version is called a concubine. Had in fact the Levite, who presumably was a member of the priestly caste, forced a virgin priestess against her will? Was this a deliberate act to try to stamp out what the Levites regarded as heresy? Why should the father of a virgin offer her to be a plaything of the men of the town according to the Biblical version? Why was this better than that the Levite should be "known" to them?

The only conclusion that I can come up with is that far from wanting to "know" the Levite, the Benjamites wanted to string him up. As for a father offering up his virgin daughter to a mob of sex hungry men, it is simply unbelievable even for that period of time. I simply do not believe the Biblical version.

I believe that what we are witnessing here is a struggle for power between the priestly/Levite and judge caste, and the multi-ethnic God/Goddess worshippers led by the Benjamites. What is more, I believe this took place during the civil war between the supporters of the betrayed House of Saul and the usurping House of David. In the Biblical version it says, "When there was no King in Israel", but in this version it says, "There was no King of Israel of the seed of Saul of the tribe of Benjamin." Clearly, therefore, this took place after Saul's death. Yuri Stoyanov and myself both agree that this version is almost certainly the original one prior to it being changed by the priests, though I have to say the priests seem to have made their case even worse in their version. It shows just how vicious religious-sectarian wars were, even then. It seems we never learn. I did actually wonder if the Levite was, in fact, Samuel. Now that would be something, wouldn't it!

When a document became frayed or damaged in ancient Israel it was the custom for a new document to be enscribed. The old document was encased and buried, as it was still considered sacred. What I suspect is that this is an old bit of scroll that was unearthed at some time and found its way into Europe in the 16th century.

I had assumed, originally, that the Benjamites had gone over to the Philistines. In the Biblical version it says that the Benjamites took wives from Shiloh, but in this version of Document 3 it says they are given wives by the people of Philistia. During our brainstorming session Yuri pointed out that the word "Philistia" might not mean the Philistines, but instead the Island of Philia or Philae in the mouth of the Nile in Egypt. On that Island was the famous Elephantine Temple to Amun and the Goddess[22], and indeed this was the time of the formation of the famous Jewish Elephantine Guard, who became the personal guard of the Pharaohs. This seemed much more likely than the Benjamites having gone off to live with their traditional enemies, the Philistines. The document says that the men of Benjamin became mighty warriors for the men of Philistia, and that is exactly what the Elephantine Guard were. They in fact became the most feared warriors of the Pharaoh's army.

The next thing was to see if Yuri and I could identify Arcassi. Again, when I had first come across this document I had assumed that it meant the mythical Arcadia, but with the identification of Philistia as Philia, we needed to look carefully at where this might be. Yuri promised to try to research this point and sure enough, a couple of weeks later he sent me an e-mail suggesting that Arcassi might be Arcas in Kurdistan, in Eastern Anatolia. One of the interesting things for anyone who watched the battles of the special forces, who together with the Kurds fought and took Iraqi Kurdistan during the second Iraqi conflict, was that, as they will no doubt have noticed, the Kurds maintained that they were Jews, before being forced to become Muslims.

Now if we were right in identifying Bethany as the people from Bithynia, which was in Northwest Anatolia and right next door to Eastern Anatolia, and if Mary of Bethany was of the House of Saul as claimed, then it looked as if we had hit the jackpot.

There was to be further confirmation of this migration from a very different source. Some years ago I had met Princess Irene Bagration, who also happens to hold a Ph.D. from the Russian Academy of Sciences in Afro-Asian Studies. She came to stay with my wife, Hermione and myself. The Bagrations had been the Ruling Family of Georgia before Georgia had been annexed by one of the Tsars, and the family became mediatised. During several days of discussion, I learnt that their superscription in their glory days had been: "Of the House of Saul, David and Bagratide." Later, for reasons that are not clear, it was changed to, "The House of David, Solomon and Bagratide." I showed Irene the County Down Document about the Benjamites and to my surprise she said, "Where did you get this? It's an old family document." Their copy is of course in Russian, probably translated via Georgian. Now I do not think that Document 3 came from Russia, so we had two sources for virtually the same document.

According to the Bagration tradition, they descend from the last Prince or Princess of the House of Saul, who had married into the House of David, but had then gone with his or her people on their migration through what is now Iraq and on into Georgia. According to Biblical sources, Michal, daughter of Saul, did indeed marry David, but then returned to her father's house during the civil war. However, according to the Biblical account she was forced to return very unwillingly to David, having in the meantime married one Phaltiel, son of Laish. "Then Ishbosheth sent and took her from her husband, even from Phaltiel the son of Laish."[23]

Had she left behind a son by David? There was unfortunately no evidence one way or another, but it looked likely.

So there appear to have been two distinct groups of Benjamite migration. The first one finished up on the Island of Philia and became employees of the Pharaohs, and the second possibly later—or maybe simply a split migrated northwards to Mesopotamia, into Anatolia and then some into modern Georgia. As with all migrations, some families or individuals would have dropped off, either because they married locals and decided to stay, or simply got fed up with moving and were happy where they were.

If this was correct, and I saw no reason to doubt it, then a group of Benjamites who had dropped off during the migration in Bithynia had formed a trading base with their brethren or co-religionists in Israel and one of them, Mary, had finished up marrying Jesus. Another group had become Princes of Georgia and had later married into the Russian Royal Family.

We had therefore found a group of people who had possibly been God-Kings in Babylon and at the very least considered that they were descended from the God Odin, who had married into a line of Jewish kings descended from both the main branches of David and Benjamin. One of these descendents, Jesus, had been proclaimed as God himself by the Pauline Church. Their descendents could indeed call themselves God-Kings. But the jigsaw puzzle was not to end there.

Chapter 4 References:

1. The First Book of Samuel Chap. 2 v. 22. It is likely that most of Samuel was written by the priest Abiather. See Enc. Brit. (1998), 15th. Edition Vol. 14, p. 933.

2. Ibid., Chap. 7 v. 15.

3. Ibid., Chap. 8 v. 5.

4. Ibid., Chap. 8 v. 6.

5. Ibid., Chap. 8 v. 11-17.

6. Ibid., Chap 8 v. 19.

7. Ibid., Chap. 10 v. 19.

8. Ibid., Chap. 10 v. 27.

9. Ibid., Chap. 10 v. 25.

10. Ibid., Chap. 12 v. 3.

11. Ibid., Chap. 15 v. 11-23.

12. Ibid., Chap. 15 v. 35.

13. Ibid., Chap. 31 v. 6.

14. Ibid., Chap. 25 v. 1.

15. The Second Book of Samuel Chap. 2 v. 8-9.

16. Judges Chap. 19 v. 24.

17. Ibid., Chap. 19 v. 25.

18. Ibid., Chap. 19 v. 28.

19. Document translated by William Montgomery (1633-1706). Publishedprivately by Georgiana Reilly, a descendent of his, circa 1820 and transcribed by J. C. Montgomery, circa 1920. He called or labelled it *The Book of Zion*. Almost certainly part of Scaliger's manuscripts— see Appendix 2. There is also a version sometimes called the Berlin Manuscript, but I am unaware of a translation.

20. Judges Chap. 2 v. 10.

21. Ibid., Chap. 2 v. 13.

22. The Temple was eventually destroyed by the Syrians.

23. II Samuel Chap. 3 v. 15-16.

Chapter 5

Some Background History

People today tend to think of ancient Israel as being one country, but for much of its life there were two kingdoms, Judea and Israel, with different kings who frequently fought against each other. The legacy of the conflict between Saul and David still persisted. During David's reign there had never been a strong centralised government. It was a kingdom in name only, with Israel in the north and Judah in the south. The King of Judah could not govern the Israelites without their consent. This had been part of David's problem. He had eventually forced the Israelites to accept a dual kingship with himself as king of both countries.

His son Solomon had to be crowned in Israel under David's own supervision, probably at the capital, Shechem.[1] "And they made Solomon the son of David king...and Israel harkened to him."

Solomon is always thought of as being wise, but the people of Israel in the north regarded him as tyrannical. When he died in 931 BC his son, Rehoboam, went to Israel to be crowned. Here he was met by the elders of Israel, who demanded redress for their grievances. Rehoboam refused to acknowledge their rights and instead sent his Judean Army against Israel.

The elders of Israel were led by Jeroboam, an Israelite general, who had had to flee to Egypt, having led a rebellion against the tyrannical Solomon. He now returned and trounced the Judeans in no uncertain terms. The combined kingdom was over, if it ever existed. Jeroboam assumed the throne of Israel and Rehoboam was left with Judah.

The throne of Israel was, to put it mildly, a dangerous sort of post to occupy. The average time in post was 11 years. There were nine separate dynasties during its 212 years of existence, one of which lasted for as little as seven days. There were some nineteen kings in all, and few of them died in their beds.

These kings even established separate temples. One in Jerusalem and one in Bethel, not to be confused with Bethlehem in Judea, established by King Jeroboam of Israel. If we look at the story of the Levite and his concubine, according to Judges Chapter 19, it says that his concubine/wife came from Beth-lehem-judah—in other words, from the town of Bethlehem in the Kingdom of Judah. This seems to have been one of the problems, as the Levite was clearly from Israel.[2] There is also a suggestion that the "E" and "J" documents were written at this time — the "J" in Judah and the "E" in Israel. If so, then one or both would have had to be hidden at the time of the Babylonian exile. My own personal opinion is that the "J" documents were written during or immediately after the Babylonian exile and that when the Jews (ex-Judea) returned under Zerubbabel, Sheshbazzar and Jeshua, they found a problem. Those Jews, who had somehow survived the holocaust of Babylonia, were not best pleased to see the Babylonians, as they saw them, returning. They had developed their own way of worship and perhaps their own scriptures.

Modern archaeology, however, tells a different story. There was no United Kingdom of Israel/Judah under David and Solomon. In fact, many scholars doubted the existence of both of these kings until a stele was found with David's name on it. During the period of Saul, David and Samuel, Jerusalem was a mudbrick village without even a wall, let alone a great fortress with a temple. There was instead a series of Canaanite city-states with individual rulers — either kings or priests. We can say, therefore, with some certainty that the real story of Saul and David is that they were kings of *"different"* cities who fought wars against each other and that David eventually won, taking a daughter of Saul as his captive bride/mistress. Samuel was probably a high priest of another city-state, possibly Ramah, who initially supported Saul and then changed allegiance and supported David. He may even have become the High Priest of Saul's city, who perhaps acted later as a spy or fifth column in Saul's city in support of David, after being dismissed by Saul!

The Northern Kingdom (Israel) developed first, some centuries later than David, based upon its olive oil, which it was able to export and thereby achieved a considerable amount of wealth. The Southern Kingdom (Judah) did not develop until the Northern Kingdom had been overrun by the Syrians and its inhabitants fled south and sought refuge in Judah.[3] The original temple was in the courtyard of King Zedekiah's palace and can still be seen today. The Great Temple of Jerusalem was first built by Zerubbabel, after the return from Babylon. Regretfully, the story of David and Solomon's Great Temple is a myth, though there may have been some sort of temple in existence. It was made up either as part of the myth during captivity or afterwards to promote the myth of "The Temple of Antiquity of Solomon".

The Kingdom of Israel lasted until about 722 BC, when the first lot of Israeli slaves were dragged off to Babylon. Many of its people escaped to the south and helped build up Judea, but some, presumably including the Benjamites of Saul's original city-state, moved north into Anatolia and some continued to Egypt and Philae. The Kingdom of Judea managed to survive until 586 BC, when it too went down in defeat to Nebuchadnezzar II (605-562 BC). Now if any religious scripts had survived it is almost certain that they would have been from Judea. In fact, the only reason the Jews of Judea survived as an entity was the relatively short time between their captivity in 582 BC and their being granted permission to return by Cyrus II (538-530 BC), less than 50 years.

Both Sheshbazzar, who started the building of the Temple, and Zerubbabel, who completed it, were princes of the House of David and both hoped, I think, to become King of the Jews. They both disappeared from history. Max Dimont suggests that they were beheaded for treason by the Persians, who would not tolerate a "king" in Judea.[4] Jeshua, on the other hand, was a Zadok priest. Zadok was the first priest supposed to have been appointed by David and has a special place in Judaism. Jeshua was crowned with a crown of silver and gold and anointed as High Priest.[5] It is interesting that Jeshua is also called "The Branch".[6] Jesus' name in Hebrew was also Jeshua, and he is also called "The Branch".

I am quite sure that this was not lost on the Jews of Jesus' time. Here was a son of David with Zadok connections, the new High Priest/King, who just as the first Jeshua had delivered them from Babylonian control, so this Jeshua would deliver them from the Romans.

The real likely scenario was as follows:

1. Saul was the King of the Northern Kingdom—Israel or a city-state that formed part of it.

2. Eli and later Samuel were high priests of a temple cult of the one God (Aten/Jahweh/Ana?—we do not know), probably based at "Ramah" in Graeco-Roman "Arimathea".

3. David was king of a small city-state in what became Judea.

4. Samuel's people wanted to become part of the successful Northern Kingdom and demanded that Saul become their king, much against Samuel's wishes. Saul's people were worshippers of more than one God, both male and female.

5. Samuel plots with the envious Southern City. When the Syrians attack a descendent of Samuel, or possibly another person called Samuel, he seizes his chance. When the Syrians overthrow the Northern Kindom some of the inhabitants flee south and help establish the Kingdom of Judea on a firm basis.

6. By the time of the return from Babylon Saul, Samuel and David are long dead, but the myths remain, to be incorporated into the *History of Israel* by the priests/kings, descendents of the house of David.

7. It was this powerful myth which produced the apocalyptic prophecies of John and Jesus.

Chapter 5 References:

1. II Chronicles Chap. 29 v. 22-23.

2. Judges Chap. 19 v. 12.

3. Secrets of the Old Testament, Channel 5 TV, documentary, 5th April, 2005.

4. Dimont, M. I. (1962) – *Jews, God and History*, p. 68, Signet Books, New York.

5. Zechariah Chap. 6 v. 11.

6. Ibid., v. 12.

Chapter 6

The Davidic Line of Septimania

In 1972 Prof. Arthur Zuckerman of Columbia University published an academic book called *A Jewish Princedom in Feudal France, 768-900*.[1] The book attracted very little attention outside of academic circles until it was mentioned casually in a best seller by Baigent, Leigh and Lincoln called *The Holy Blood and the Holy Grail*.

Since then a variety of authors have referred to it, but few if any seem to have actually read it or, if they have, understood it. One of the problems for the non-specialist is that many of the documents are in Medieval Latin and Hebrew and indeed there are so many scholarly notes to each page that it requires a considerable determination to work one's way through the book. This by no means is a criticism, on the contrary it shows a degree of research and accuracy that I find most commendable.

In order to pursue this work Prof. Zuckerman had to consult a considerable amount of archival material, not only in the National Archives in France, but also in departmental archives in Toulouse, Perpignan, Carcassonne, Montpellier, Nîmes, Marseilles, Avignon, Lyons, Troyes and many other locations. Having spent several weeks myself trawling for documents in the lower Normandy area, I can testify to the amount of work entailed.

There is little point in my trying to reproduce in one chapter all the work that Prof. Zuckerman has put in to his book, but as much of what he has found is related directly to the theme of this book and indeed confirms much of my own research. It is therefore necessary for me to give in this chapter enough information from Prof. Zuckerman's book so that readers may appreciate the importance of this work and how it interrelates with the information given in other chapters.

According to the Bible, the Babylonian king, Evil-Merodakh (562-560 BC), released the Jewish king in exile, Yehoiakhin, from prison, admitted him into his House (Court) and eventually elevated him above all other vassal kings in Babylon and made him head of all the Jews in his empire. Yehoiakhin's descendent, Zerubbabel, whom we mentioned in the previous chapter, eventually becomes Cyrus II's satrap in Judea (see Chap. 5). There then followed a succession of Jewish rulers or Exilarchs from this same family during both the subsequent Seleucid and Parthian dynasties of Babylonia. The later neo-Persian kings conferred total authority on the Exilarch and he became a member of their Council of State. His official title was "Rosh-golah" (or Resh-gulata), meaning "Head of the Exile".[2] You will remember from Chap. 5 that any attempt to establish a King of the Jews based in Jerusalem had been swiftly dealt with and Jeshua had only been crowned as "High Priest" of the line of Zadok. The Exilarch was a satrap, not a king. Following the unsuccessful rebellion against the Romans, the Exilarch had returned to Baghdad, possibly either Jesus himself or one of his sons.

Mohammed had died in 632 AD and Abu Bekr had been chosen to succeed him with the title of Caliph. His seat of power was Medina. It was, however, after the Arab conquest of Persia in 637 AD and the establishment of the Caliphate in Baghdad that the Exilarchy became almost autonomous. The "Prince" (note the title) of the exile was the representative of all Jews in the Caliphate. He was a member of the Caliph's *diwan*, or cabinet, and together with the Catholicos of the Nestorian Christian Church, was one of the highest dignitaries of the Islamic empire. For just a short time all three monotheistic religions lived in harmony. It is noteworthy that we can thank the Nestorian Christians for preserving the non-canonical works that are referred to in this book.

The Exilarch could appoint "judges" who were his representatives in all local and provincial centres of Jewry. He exercised complete jurisdiction over all Jews in the Caliphate. He was, in effect, the exiled monarch of all Jews based in Baghdad, but he had greater powers than any King of the Jews had ever had. He was not only the head of the judiciary, but the spiritual head and commander of the Jewish warriors, should the Caliph call upon them.

The Exilarch, who had to have Davidic descent, was elected at a public assembly of all Jews in Babylon, presided over by the Geonim, the heads of the academies of Sura and Pumbeditha. The Caliph then had to confirm this election, for which the newly elected Exilarch had to pay a large sum of money. This continued well into the 9th and 10th centuries. The Exilarch had his own "Palace" in an area of Baghdad[3] and when he went out, had runners running before him crying, "Make way for the Son of David."

In Europe, this pinnacle of Exilarch princely authority and power coincided with the reigns of Charles Martel (717-741), Pepin (741-768), Charlemagne (768-814), and Louis the Debonair (814-840).

There had also been another Jewish institution in the old Roman Empire. This was the Patriarch or Nasi, based in Palestine. This Patriarch also claimed Davidic descent via Hillel the Elder. Notwithstanding the claim that Hillel was of Davidic descent, Israel Lévi found that this claim arose almost two hundred years after Hillel's death and had no basis in reality.[4] When the Roman Empire threw most of the Jews out of Palestine, it found an easy way to both keep tabs on a "troublesome people" and to tax them without having to do the dirty work themselves. After the Roman Empire became Christianised it continued to recognise the Patriarch as supreme authority over the Jews in the Roman Empire. To Origen (3rd Cent. AD), the Jewish Patriarch seemed the same as a king. The Patriarch, however, was supranational, having legal, administrative and fiscal authority over all Jews within the Empire.

It was his prerogative to collect the Jewish poll tax (Aurum Coronarium, or d'mei k'lila). Not all of the taxes collected found their way to Rome. The Patriarch was allowed to keep some to maintain the dignity of his office and the support of poor students. The Patriarchy was suppressed in 425 AD, exactly 100 years after the Council of Nicea.

In Europe, Jewish communities had already been established as early as 6 AD, when King Archelaus was exiled to Vienna. Herod Antipas was also banished to Lyons some thirty-three years later and we know that Herod himself had a villa near to Marseilles. Interestingly enough, many Jews came as members of the Roman Army, which means that at least some must have joined the Legions in preference for joining the *Diaspora*. There is indeed mention of a Jewish Legion and it is possible. After all, Josephus had "converted" to Roman ideas. Josephus had been born Joseph ben Matthias in about 37-38 AD in Jerusalem. He was born into a priestly aristocratic family. By the age of 14 he was being consulted by the high priests in the temple about Jewish Law (as had Jesus, according to Biblical sources). At the age of 16 he made a three-year sojourn in the desert with the hermit Bannus. Returning, he joined the Pharisees. In 64 AD he was sent on a mission to Rome to help release some priests imprisoned there. He was introduced to Poppaea Sabina, the second wife of Nero, and became friendly with the Imperial Family. Subsequently, he espoused the cause of Vespasian and when Vespasian became Emperor, Josephus was adopted into the Imperial Family and became Josephus Flavius—Flavius being the family name of Vespasian. He later went with Vespasian to Alexandria, where he married.

Rome made a point of recruiting auxiliaries from its conquered peoples, forming them into tight-knit groups of soldiers. I see no reason, therefore, why there should not have been a Jewish Legion. They, however, never served in their "home country" for obvious reasons, and it is not unlikely that they would have been sent to Southern Europe. The Jews of the Roman Empire in Europe were expected to fulfill curial duties, the same as any other Roman, and in a decree of December, 331 Constantine actually has to exempt certain Jews from having to fulfill these duties (hieri, archisynagogi and patres synagogae—translated roughly as Priests, Heads of Synagogues and the Fathers of the Synagogues).[5]

In Visigothic regions, Jews are specifically thought of as "Romans". Both the Breviarium of Alaric II and the Lex Romana Burgundionum of Gundobar (see Chapter 1), specifically refer to the Jews as "Roman". One of the problems for the early Christian Church in Europe was that Jews and Christians mixed together socially and frequently married each other. The Church disliked this, as it often meant one partner converting to Judaism, so they forbade these wherever possible.

When I first came across Document No. 2, mentioned in Chapter 2, I presumed that this showed that the Merovingians had been descended from Mary of Bethany and Jesus, and had been puzzled as to why the Merovingians kings had dealt so badly with the Jews. Clovis I had been the first to launch what amounted to a pogrom, and Dagobert in 633 gave the Jews a choice of conversion or exile. It was not until I was in the process of unraveling the antecedents of the Gothic kings that I realised that in fact the Merovingians dynasty did *not* descend from the Elchasais and the Davidic line, and therefore felt no allegiance to any Jewish ancestry. Indeed, they were probably willing servants of the Church because they may have felt that their Royalty was not as good as that of the descendents of Ataulf and Maria, even though Clovis married a female descendent of Ataulf and Maria. (See Chap. 1.)

When Duke Paul, sent to quell a local rebellion in Nîmes, threw in his lot with the locals and then had himself proclaimed king and renounced his allegiance to King Wamba (672-680), the Jews of Septimania sided with Paul. In order to pay for his campaign, Paul looted the Christian Churches and there was a general movement in the area away from Christianity, towards Judaism.

His success was short-lived. Wamba led his army through Gascony and Catalonia, through the Pyrenees, took Narbonne and captured Paul at Nîmes. He had Paul's eyes gouged out and sentenced Paul and his associates to life imprisonment. On his way home he expelled all Jews from Narbonne. By 720 AD the victories of Wamba had been nullified by the advance of the Saracens and the capture of Narbonne by Al-Samh, and by the end of August, 725 AD the final remnant of the once proud Gothic Kingdom of Septimania and Toulouse had fallen to the Saracens.

We must now turn our attention to the contentious issue of the fall of Narbonne to Pepin in 759 AD. Until Prof. Zuckerman's work the general prevailing view was that the remaining Visigoths in Narbonne had made a deal with Pepin, whereby they would slaughter the Arab garrison and open Narbonne to Pepin in return for self-rule. At least one authority before Zuckerman, namely Pückert, has attacked the veracity of these chronicles written by a 9th century Goth monk, known later as St. Benedict, but born Witiza of Aniane, son of the Gothic Count Maguelonne. He wrote the chronicles *Annals of Aniane*, in which the whole action became the actions of Christian Goths, as opposed to Jews. (Well, he would, wouldn't he!)[6]

However, there exists another version that takes the form of a Latin Romance, which is supported by both Hebrew and Papal documents and that describes in considerable detail how the Jews went out secretly, met Pepin and agreed to hand over the Citadel of Narbonne in return for their being given independence under their own ruler. Aquitaine was virtually independent and the nobility of Septimania were quite as likely to side with the Saracens as with the emerging Pepinid/Charlemagnic dynasty.

The caliphate too, was in a state of change. The once great Umayyad dynasty had gone down in defeat to Abu'l Abbas, who had overthrown the Caliph of Dasmascus in 750 AD. The sole survivor of this dynasty, Abd al-Rahman, had fled to Spain and declared that this was the "Real Caliphate". There was now a permanent split between the new Abbasis Caliphate in Damascus and the old Caliphate now based in Cordova. This created a number of strange alliances. Anti-Umayyad Walis (local officials) made common cause with the Franks, whilst anti-Carolingian Christian Lords allied themselves with the Umayyad dynasty. The old Gothic nobility were, in fact, totally opposed to the Franks.[7] This allowed Pepin to open negotiations with the new Abbasid Caliphate, and who better to do this than the Jews, whose Exilarch was now the Grand Vizier at the Court of the Abbasid Caliph in Damascus. In fact, the Caliph had given his daughter in marriage to his Grand Vizier.

It is also important to realise that during their conquests of 719-720, the Saracens had, upon conquering a town, turned it over to Jews to manage. Al -Makkari says: "Whenever the Muslims conquered a town, it was left in the custody of the Jews."[8] The consequence of placing Jews in charge of administrating towns was that some towns became all Jewish. Even the capital of the Spanish Caliphate, Cordova had a majority population of Jews as late as the middle of the 9th century. Tarragona was known as the "City of the Jews" and even in the 12th century Muslims still referred to Granada as "Jewish" Granada.

The Jews, therefore, rose and opened the gates of the city of Narbonne to Pepin. In return they were given complete independence. Abraham ibn Daud takes up the tale: "Then King Charles (he mistook the date of Charlemagne's accession to the throne, as he was writing in 1160) sent to the King of Babylon (Caliph) requesting that he dispatch one of his Jews of the seed of royalty of the House of David. He hearkened and sent him one from there, a magnate and sage, Rabbi Makhir by name. And (the king) settled him in Narbonne, the capital city, and planted him there, and gave him great possession (ahuzah) there at the time he captured it from the Ishmalites (Muslims). And he (the Makhir) took to wife..."[9]

Historically we know that in 765 Pepin sent a mission to Baghdad, now the centre of the Abbasid Caliphate and that this mission returned in 768, accompanied by the Ambassador of Caliph Al-Mansur. In order to understand what happened next it is necessary to understand what had happened in Baghdad. The problem was that the previous Exilarch had married a Persian Princess, Izdunadad, whose sister had married either the Caliph or his son. The Exilarch was therefore related to the Caliph's family. The problem was whether or not the Persian Princess had been manumitted and converted to Judaism before bearing the Exilarch's sons. Because the Caliph wished Izdunadad's son to be recognised as Exilarch, one of the "pure" line from Bustanai, the earlier Exilarch was effectively dethroned and agreed to go to the West and establish an Exilarchy in Narbonne. This was Natronai b. Habibai (Habibai is another form of Bustani).

In this way, the problem of succession in the Exilarch of Baghdad was overcome. The Jews of Narbonne got the leader, the Caliph had an ally in Frankish territories and Pepin was assured of friendly relations with Baghdad and obtained a set of allies in the Jews of Narbonne to counter any ambitions from his own vassals.

I cannot do better than to quote the last paragraph of Chapter 4 of Prof. Zuckerman's book. He says that there is evidence that Pepin set up a Jewish Princedom in southern Frankia in the year 768. "Its ruler or governor (Nasi, patriarch) was Natronai-Makhir, a former Exilarch of the Jews in Baghdad and scholar-prince of the royal House of David. In this capacity he would legitimise the autonomous existence of Jews in Frankia, living under their own law, by conferring his *divinely-ordained* authority on local community leaders. Both Abbasid Caliph and the Carloingian king collaborated in this project. The Church was outraged. Pope Stephen III reacted violently when apprised of the actual cession of allodial lands to the Jewish Nasi."[10]

His language was extreme even by the standards of the day. "We have been distressed to the point of death...(*The rights of the Jews*)(11) ...even though sworn to by God Himself and transmitted to these unbelievers and their wicked fathers, were rightly abrogated as punishment for the crucifixion of the Saviour... And what agreement has the Temple of God with idols?"[12]

The Merovingian kings had become anti-Semitic, and when the main branch of the Visigothic kings, who were not descended from the direct line of Ataulf and Maria, converted from Arian Christianity to Roman Catholicism, they too became anti-Semitic—in fact, even worse than the Merovingians. Receswinth (649-672) and Erwig (680-687) had made the Jews life difficult, and the worst of all, Egica (687-702) had reduced Jews to slavery, taken their infants from them forcibly to be brought up in Christian homes and had them forcibly married to Christians. Their lands had been taken and they had been taxed for the privilege.

All in all, one can understand why the Jews in Southern France and the Spanish March should have been so keen to help Pepin in return for a ruler and laws of their own. Why Pepin should have been so keen is not quite so obvious. It is probable that he had little option. Many nobles did not like his dynasty ascending the Frankish throne—after all, as Mayors of the Palace they had ranked lower than many of their new subjects.

In many cases Pepin and Charlemagne were merely returning to the Jews lands that had been taken from them either by the Church or by those acting at the Church's behest.

What now happened is of immense significance. Natronai-Makhir married Alda, the sister of Pepin and daughter of Charles Martel. It is also likely that Al-Makir had already a family in Baghdad, who either came with him or joined him later and it seems that one of these daughters married Charlemagne. A daughter of the marriage between Alda and Natronai, Judith, married King Louis the debonair. The result was the formation of two separate lines of descent from the House of Arnulf (Pepin's family name) and the House of David. Pepin had, by doing this, realised his House's ambition to establish it as a successor to the biblical kings of Israel and consequently, they would no longer have to pretend to their inherited *divinely-ordained* right to rule. This, perhaps, was the raison d'etre for both Pepin and Charlemagne. For barely had Natronai-Makhir been established than Pepin the Short died and was succeeded by Charles, later to be known as Charlemagne.

Charlemagne, however, not only confirms Pepin's agreement but seemingly goes even further. The Nasis are ennobled by being given the highest titles in the land and Charlemagne allows members of his court to convert to Judaism—a thing previously banned. His bishops are, of course, outraged and even more so when Charlemagne takes one of the Nasi's daughters as a wife. I use the word wife, but Charlemagne actually had at least four known wives and at least seven concubines and treated the children of each equally. I am of the tentative opinion that Hildegard was the daughter of the Nasi. She was the mother of Bertha, who married the famous poet Angilbert. He wrote a number of poems praising both Charlemagne as "David" and his wife as the "daughter of David". She would obviously have had a Jewish name apart from Hildegard, possibly Esther.

The Jewish document confirming Charlemagne's grant reads as follows:

> *"In 791 a delegation of ten men headed by an Isaac, peti-*
> *tioned Charlemagne in the name of the Jewish 'king', whose*
> *seat was in Narbonne, to make permanent the institution of a*
> *Jewish Monarchy there; Charlemagne confirmed this king-*
> *ship as a permanent institution for an annual payment of 70*
> *marks silver."*

Charlemagne was able to do this once he had been proclaimed Emperor, but to be proclaimed Emperor he needed something more. His line was a line of usurpers. Marrying into the Davidic line certainly helped, but if he could become the "Guardian of the Holy Sepulchre", that would show that his house's usurpation had God's blessing. So he sent Isaac (William) to Baghdad to talk to the new Caliph, in whose domain the so-called Holy Sepulchre resided. William was, of course, a relative of the Caliph and spoke Arabic as well as Hebrew, Latin and French. Two days before Charlemagne's coronation, a priest called Zechariah arrived in Rome with the Banner and Keys of Jerusalem and Mount Zion. Temporarily, at least Charles was Guardian of part of Jerusalem and the Holy City, including the Holy Sepulchre. No wonder the Makhir got his kingdom (for the full story, see Zuckerman, p. 186-191).

One of the interesting small points is that Alcuin, the great Medieval philosopher and teacher, referred to Charlemagne as "Charles of the House of David", or sometimes simply as David (David amate Deo).

I have compiled the following genealogical tables from the information contained in Prof. Zuckerman's book, plus some researches of my own:

The Makhirs of Septimania (Part 1)

Natronai-Makhir

= 1st marriage in Baghdad

Daughter (Hildegard) = Charlemagne

****

DESCENT FROM CHARLEMAGNE (13)

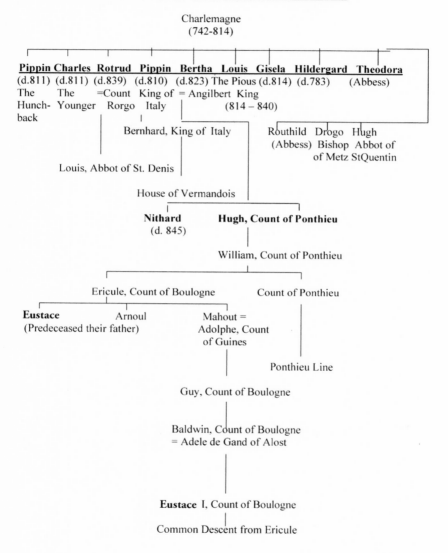

Charlemagne
(742-814)

Pippin **Charles** **Rotrud** **Pippin** **Bertha** **Louis** **Gisela** **Hildergard** **Theodora**
(d.811) (d.811) (d.839) (d.810) (d.823) The Pious (d.814) (d.783)   (Abbess)
The   The   =Count   King of = Angilbert King
Hunch- Younger Rorgo   Italy   (814 – 840)
back

Bernhard, King of Italy

Routhild Drogo Hugh
(Abbess) Bishop Abbot of
         of Metz StQuentin

Louis, Abbot of St. Denis

House of Vermandois

Nithard   **Hugh, Count of Ponthieu**
(d. 845)

William, Count of Ponthieu

Ericule, Count of Boulogne   Count of Ponthieu

Eustace   Arnoul   Mahout =
(Predeceased their father)   Adolphe, Count
                                  of Guines

Ponthieu Line

Guy, Count of Boulogne

Baldwin, Count of Boulogne
= Adele de Gand of Alost

Eustace I, Count of Boulogne

Common Descent from Ericule

The Makhirs of Septimania (Part 2)

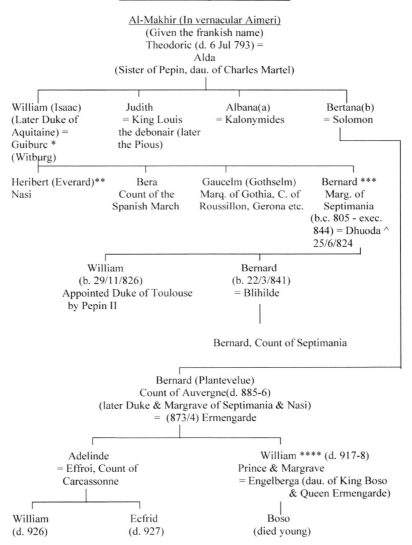

Al-Makhir (In vernacular Aimeri)
(Given the frankish name)
Theodoric (d. 6 Jul 793) =
Alda
(Sister of Pepin, dau. of Charles Martel)

William (Isaac)
(Later Duke of
Aquitaine) =
Guiburc *
(Witburg)

Judith
= King Louis
the debonair (later
the Pious)

Albana(a)
= Kalonymides

Bertana(b)
= Solomon

Heribert (Everard)**
Nasi

Bera
Count of the
Spanish March

Gaucelm (Gothselm)
Marq. of Gothia, C. of
Roussillon, Gerona etc.

Bernard ***
Marg. of
Septimania
(b.c. 805 - exec.
844) = Dhuoda ^
25/6/824

William
(b. 29/11/826)
Appointed Duke of Toulouse
by Pepin II

Bernard
(b. 22/3/841)
= Blihilde

Bernard, Count of Septimania

Bernard (Plantevelue)
Count of Auvergne(d. 885-6)
(later Duke & Margrave of Septimania & Nasi)
= (873/4) Ermengarde

Adelinde
= Effroi, Count of
Carcassonne

William **** (d. 917-8)
Prince & Margrave
= Engelberga (dau. of King Boso
& Queen Ermengarde)

William
(d. 926)

Ecfrid
(d. 927)

Boso
(died young)

The above genealogical tree has been produced by me from the information in Professor Arthur Zuckerman's book.

(a) & (b) It is not clear from the literature as to whether Bertrana married Solomon & Albana married the Kalonymides, or vice versa. It simply says daughter of, without indicating her name.

*   A non-Christian from beyond the sea.

**   Opposed Agobard and was blinded by Lothar.

^ Sister or sister-in-law of Emperor, Louis the Debonnair.

***   Count of Barcelona, later Camerarius (Chamberlain) to Louis and protector of infant Charles. Nasi after the blinding of Heribert. Most important person after the Emperor. Septimania called a "Kingdom" at this time. Cousin of Eudo of Orleans.

**** William founded an institution of Jewish learning in what became the Abbey of Cluny. After his death he was "Christianised" by the Church and became known as William the Pious.

Bernard Plantevelue was known as "Hairy Foot".

With the end of the line of the original Makhirs, the collateral branch of the Makhirs—the Kalonymides of Lucca—were asked in 917 by King Charles (893-923) to come to the Narbonne as Nasis. The first of this line was known in Hebrew as Rabbi Moses the Elder, his son's cognomen was "En-Kalonymos". This line continued at least until the 14th century. In 1246 we find a Charter signed in Hebrew (Moumet Judeu d'Nerpo) and sealed with the Seal of the Lion Rampant of the House of Judah and a six pointed star, and in 1307-8 we find references to "Momet Tauros—King of the Jews".

The name "Makhir", or its Frankish form "Aimeri", is not really a proper name but more of a title, indicating someone who is the spiritual as well as civil (and often military) head of the Jewish people in that area, particularly in the Aquitaine region, where many members of the nobility married into this family or gave their daughters in marriage to the Makhirs. It is very likely also that several noble families converted to Judaism or, at the very least, accepted it. For example, in the Diet of Pitres in 864 Pippin II of Aquitaine was accused of apostasy to paganism (of the Norsemen?). It seems more likely that he became a Jew. (Having said that, he may have been a member of the Ulvungar dynasty, whom we shall be dealing with in a later chapter, though I have yet found a connection.)

Theodoric was Al-Makhir as was William (Isaac Al-Makhir) and Heribert would have Al-Makhir before being blinded, at which point his brother Bernard became Al-Makhir. Equally, when Bernard (Plantevelue) became the Nasi he would have become Al-Makhir or Aimeri, as would his son Bernard and when Rabbi Moses the Elder was asked to become Nasi by Charles, he would have been known as "Aimeri" in the vernacular. We can say, therefore, with a fair degree of certainty that Aimeri de Thouars, one of William the Conqueror's companions, was clearly a descendent of the Makhirs and leader of his people in that area of Aquitaine.[14]

It is interesting to note how many Jews commanded the various armies of not only Charlemagne and Louis, but also of other kingdoms. William, the son of the first Makhir, was continuously at war fighting the Saracens or indeed, Christian rebels, against the Emperors. He was in charge of the whole of the Spanish March. Another of the great Jewish scholar-army commanders was Abu-Ibrahim Samuel ben Joseph Halevi ibn Nagrela (993-1056). He was the Nagid of the Jews of the Kingdom of Granada and the Grand Vizier, or highest official second only to the King/Caliph himself. Between 1038-1056 there were only two years that he did not lead his troops on campaign. He was also a great scholar who wrote out not only a faithful copy of the Hebrew Bible in his own hand, but also a concordance to the Bible. He also wrote a halakhic text himself, was a known poet and headed a Talmudic academy. He was succeeded by his son Joseph. This was only ten years before the battle of Hastings.[15]

With the end of the first line of Makhirs, the line of Kalonymides takes over. We can pick up the line from Aymeri I, Viscount of Narbonne (1080-1105) and from Aimeri de Thouars, who was a "Companion" of William the Conqueror and led many of his own troops on the left flank of William's forces at Hastings. This line can be seen to have continued in France and Germany, even after the expulsion of the Jews in 1306, with the leader of medieval Hasidim, Samuel ben Kalonymos (The Hasid) and his two sons, Judah ben Samuel and Eleazar ben Judah Kalonymos. Their special work was the esoteric "Sefer Hasidim".[16]

So far, in Europe, we have an Odonic Line, a line of the House of David via the Elchasaic dynasty, a line of Benjamite and House of Saul, also via the Elchasaic dynasty, and another via the Benjamite Diaspora—and we have now shown that there existed another Davidic line, via the Makhirs of Septimania.

Chapter 6 References:

1. Zuckerman, A.J. (1972) – *A Jewish Princedom in Feudal France 768-900*, Columbia University Press, New York & London.

2. Ibid., p. 1.

3. Ibid., p. 2. See also Albright, W. F. (1942) – *King Joiachin in Exile*, The Biblical Archaeologist, Vol. V, p. 50-53.

4. Lévi, I. (1895) – *L'origine davidique de Hillel*, Revue des études juives, XXXI, p. 211 and (1896) XXXIII, p. 143-144. See also Zuckerman, *op. cit.* p. 3.

5. *Codex Theodosianus* (315) – eds. Mommsen and Meyer, Vol. 1 p.887.

6. For the whole argument see Zuckerman, *op. cit.* Chap. 2. Also Pückert, W. (1953) – Aniane und Gellone, p. 104-110.

7. Dupont, A., cited by Zuckerman, *op. cit.* p. 43, note 13.

8. Al-Makkari, A ibn M. – *History of the Mohammedan Dynasties in Spain*, p. 280-282 & p. 531 note 18, cited by Zuckerman, *op. cit.* p. 47.

9. Daud, ibn A. (1160-61) – *Sefer Seder haKabbalah*, Addendum, Adler's MS no. 2237, Jewish Theological Seminary of America. Cited by Zuckerman, *op. cit.* p. 59.

10. Zuckerman, *op. cit.* p. 100-101.

11. My italics.

12. Zuckerman, *op. cit.* p. 50.

13. Platts, B. (1985) – *Scottish Hazard*, Vol. 1, p. 38, Procter Press, London; Also Montgomery, H. (2002) – *Montgomery Millennium*, p. 2-3, Megatrend, Belgrade & London; Also *Karl der Grosse*; Also McKitterick, R. (1983) – *The Frankish Kingdoms under the Carolingians 781-987*, p. 349-367, Longman, UK.

14. Zuckerman, op. cit. p. 367. See also Montgomery, H. (2004) – *The Norman Families and the Conquest of England*, p. 33.

15. Schirmann, J. (1951) – *Samuel Hannagid, the Man, the Soldier, the Politician*, Jewish Social Studies, XII, p. 99-126.

16. Encyclopaedia Britannica under "Hasidim".

Chapter 7

The Ulvungar Dynasty

We finished Chapter 1 with the descent of Harald Hylthetan from Rhoes the Weoôulgeot. However, Harald Hylthetan was known by another name, that of Herioldus Brochus. "Lode" is Low German for *scion,* while "Brocus" is Latin for "prominent tooth or tusk" and one of the greatest rulers of Denmark, whose existence is well document-ed in Saxo Grammaticus and the Chronicles of Lethra, bore the name Harald Hildetand (or Hilditønn), which in Latin is Herioldus Brocus. Much has been written about Ragnar Lothbroc, the brave snake-killer of the Scandinavian Sagas and the words "son of Lothbroc" occurs on many occasions to denote descent from this fabled fairy-tale warrior. In the Sagas this is explained as an expression used to describe the *hairy trousers* he is supposed to have worn when killing the serpent. Regretfully, like most of the Sagas this has no basis in reality.

The Irish called the descendents of Herioldus "Leather-coats" (or Lodebrochus) because of the leather coats they used instead of chain mail, in cold weather. In Asser's *Life of King Alfred,* in an account of the battle in Devonshire in 878 AD, he uses the term Lodebrochi (gen-itive of Lodebrochus). The story describes the battle in which Ulf (or Olaf), the King of the Danes, was killed and his banner of the Raven, (symbol of Odin) was captured by Alfred. The banner had been embroidered by the daughter's of Lothbroc—"Filiae videlicet Lodebrochi".

All descendents of the House of Brocus would have had the right to call themselves "Brochi" or, more familiarly, "Lothbrochi". Harald had two sons, each of whom in turn became King of Denmark; Godfrid who ruled between 804-810 AD and Halfdan, who ruled from 810 to 812 AD.

In Genealogy I, I have shown the descendents of Godfrid. Godfrid (Gudrod or Goder) was king of most of modern-day Denmark. He was killed whilst preparing an expedition against Charlemagne in 810. There was a scramble for power and in the fighting that ensued, Godfrid's sons, Horic and Olaf, killed Anulo, the eldest son of Halfdan.[1]

Anulo's younger brothers, Harald and Ragnar (Ragbinfridus), then appealed to the Emperor for support in getting back their lands, but Ragnar seems to have left Denmark later on.

At this point, it is best if I deal with the matter of the so-called "Sagas". In my book *The Norman Families and the Conquest of England*, I have gone into some detail as to why I regard them as totally fictitious and the product of a drunken, devious brain. Ever since Lair, writing in 1885[2], a number of historians have come out against them. Today, most historians who have done their homework will not use Snorre (the Author of the Sagas) as a reliable source. Like much of the Bible, the Sagas were written many years after the events portrayed in them and there are so many obvious mistakes, that they cannot be relied upon.[3]

Godfrid, Chief of Ulster in 835 (see Gen. 1), was, according to the Three Fragments[4], the son of Ragnaill and father of King Ingvar. *The Annuls of Fulda*, on the other hand, say he was the brother of king Horic, "Horic Regem Danorum et Gudurm fratis ejus." This is unlikely, as otherwise Godfrid would have had a son with the same name, something that simply was not done at that time. Godfrid was chief of Fingall and the Isles in 835.

The Three Fragments, a manuscript preserved in the Burgundian Library in Brussels, contains this passage amongst others: "Amhlaeibh (Olaf) went to Erin to Lochlann to wage war on the Lochlanns, and to aid his father Godfridh." This war took place in 872, at a time when the forces of Denmark were heavily involved in trying to conquer England.

Again, Snorre reckons that Halfdan was amongst the petty kings, with a fantastic pedigree, from the ancient kings of Upsala. In fact, Halfdan was King of Westfold and Northumberland (he was killed at Strangford Lough in 877) and father of Harald Fairhair, later King of Norway (d. 933 AD). This is also confirmed from another source. Whilst I was investigating the pedigree of HRH Princess Elizabeth of Yugoslavia (Kneginja Jelisaveta Karadjordjevic), she sent me a pedigree showing her descent from Rurik and which happens to show the identical pedigree to the one in Genealogy I & II, shown hereafter.

Whilst there is no supportive evidence for Snorre's claims, there is plenty of evidence to show that Halfdan the Black was the son of Ragnvald Heiôumhaerri, King of Westfold, son of Godfrid, King of Denmark, son of Herioldus Brochus.

Halfdan's victory over his brother Godfrid and his nephew Olaf (Ingvar's brother) brought Westfold and other parts of South Norway under his control. This battle took place in 872 and Halfdan's son Harald, he of the Fairhair, was too young to accompany his father on campaign. There exists a story of Harald proposing to Princess Ragnhild of Denmark, the daughter of the younger King Horic. However, as Halfdan's wife was known to have been called "Ragnhild", it is likely that, once again, we are faced with a silly mistake and that, in fact, she was his mother.

When St. Anscharius visited Olaf (brother of Horic and Raghnaill) in 850 AD, the elder King Horic sent a letter of introduction to King Olaf of Birka, his brother, in order to help the saint's mission. This helps us to fix Olaf as living in Birka around 850.

Godfrid (of Ulster and Westfold—see Gen. I) had two sons, Olaf and Ingvar, who each became King of Dublin. In the Irish annals they are called Amhlaeibh and Imhar, but the Saxon Chronicles calls them Hinguar and Ubba. The Sagas call them the "bastard sons of Ragnar Lodbrok". They certainly could be called sons of the House of Brocus, and if one regards Raghnaill, King of Dublin, their grandfather, as *a Ragnar Lothbroc*, then I suppose there is a certain truth in the statement, but whether they were legitimate or illegitimate I have not the vaguest idea. I rather suspect that this is just envy speaking.

What follows is the first of the Ulvungar Dynasty Genealogies. There is more than one name for this dynasty. It is sometimes called the Ynglingeætt dynasty, from "ætt", meaning family and "yngling", meaning youngster—but I prefer Ulvungar.

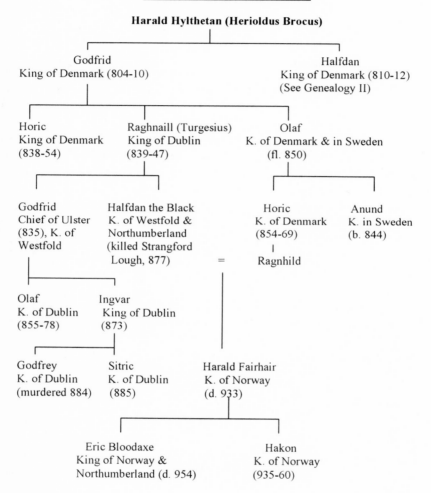

Genealogy I
Dynasty of Ulvungar
House of Lothbrook (Or Brocus)

Harald Hylthetan (Herioldus Brocus)

Godfrid
King of Denmark (804-10)

Halfdan
King of Denmark (810-12)
(See Genealogy II)

Horic
King of Denmark
(838-54)

Raghnaill (Turgesius)
King of Dublin
(839-47)

Olaf
K. of Denmark & in Sweden
(fl. 850)

Godfrid
Chief of Ulster
(835), K. of
Westfold

Halfdan the Black
K. of Westfold &
Northumberland
(killed Strangford
Lough, 877)

Horic
K. of Denmark
(854-69)

Anund
K. in Sweden
(b. 844)

= Ragnhild

Olaf
K. of Dublin
(855-78)

Ingvar
King of Dublin
(873)

Godfrey
K. of Dublin
(murdered 884)

Sitric
K. of Dublin
(885)

Harald Fairhair
K. of Norway
(d. 933)

Eric Bloodaxe
King of Norway &
Northumberland (d. 954)

Hakon
K. of Norway
(935-60)

Whilst I was doing the research for this book I sent a copy of the Genealogy to Niven Sinclair, Chairman of the Clan Sinclair Trust, who had helped me with a number of queries I had had. One of the problems that I have had in dealing with material from Scandinavian sources, is that everyone wants to claim famous people as their own and disown those of whom they disapprove. So various historical characters such as Rolf, the ancestor of the Norman Dynasty, is claimed by Norway, Sweden and Denmark. I have no axe to grind one way or another. Indeed, I find the whole thing absurd, as the present kingdoms did not come into existence until much later. The classical writers referred to all Scandinavians as either Northmen or Danes quite indiscriminately. One of Niven's colleagues in Norway wrote back with and interesting story.

It goes like this: "Norway had been ruled as one kingdom prior to Harald Hårfagre, Fairhair, but that was 200 years ago under kings belonging to the Ynglingeætt [see above], the Swedish branch of Njård Vana, who had a son, Frøy, with his sister. Frøy had the punt-name (cognomen) Yngve, meaning youngster, and from him came the kings both of Sweden and Norway. Originally, the Njård family had come to Denmark and later Sweden with the *Odinpeople*, who had fled from the Roman army on its way through Georgia to Asterbistan about 200 AD."[5] This, I thought, was a remarkable legend, which had been kept alive in Norway, and although it was not exactly the same as that described in Chapter 1, it was so near, except that events had been telescoped, that I was dumbfounded. The gentleman in question did not agree with me as regards certain other matters, which we shall come on to later, but his outline story was quite remarkable in that a folk memory had confirmed my hypothesis and research.

Effectively, what this story shows is that the Odinpeople (Kassites) had fled from somewhere (Mesopotamia), finished up in Sweden, and ultimately called the Goths. Later a second migration, now mixed with the Benjamite and Elchasaite peoples, had fled north again and founded the Ulvungar dynasty of Scandinavia. These two events had been telescoped into one legend, as often happens, and the memory of the persecutions of the Goths by the Roman Army in the 3rd century was now remembered as the reason for their fleeing north. Of such small things are great events remembered.

While I am on the subject, let me make a point here about the Vikings. They were neither uncultured nor illiterate. They had a wonderful culture of their own and a rich oral tradition, and a script of their own (Runic, which, by the way, bears a remarkable resemblance to the Cuneiform Script of Babylon). They have been given a very bad name by the monks who, by and large, wrote the chronicles. From the Vikings point of view, however, they were attacking these hated priests and the more they killed the better. Yes, they raided and despoiled churches and monasteries and took all they could of booty, but it is noticeable that whilst they took captives of the ordinary people, they generally killed priests. It is also interesting that when they were beaten in battle, they were often allowed to keep their gains in territory if they converted. Indeed, the Church urged this on the various Christian kings. The Church wanted to extend its power and control any way it could.

Genealogy II
Dynasty of Ulvungar
House of Lothbrook (Descent from Halfdan – See Genealogy I)

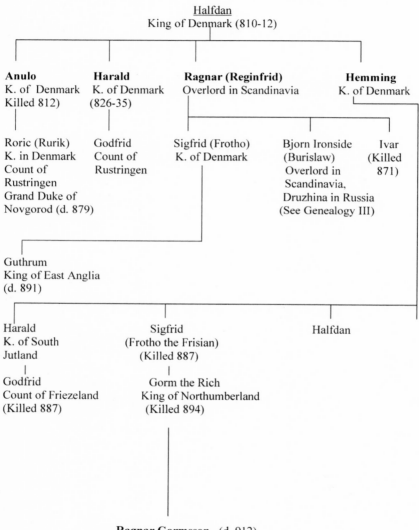

Halfdan
King of Denmark (810-12)

Anulo
K. of Denmark
Killed 812)

Harald
K. of Denmark
(826-35)

Ragnar (Reginfrid)
Overlord in Scandinavia

Hemming
K. of Denmark

Roric (Rurik)
K. in Denmark
Count of
Rustringen
Grand Duke of
Novgorod (d. 879)

Godfrid
Count of
Rustringen

Sigfrid (Frotho)
K. of Denmark

Bjorn Ironside
(Burislaw)
Overlord in
Scandinavia,
Druzhina in Russia
(See Genealogy III)

Ivar
(Killed
871)

Guthrum
King of East Anglia
(d. 891)

Harald
K. of South
Jutland

Sigfrid
(Frotho the Frisian)
(Killed 887)

Halfdan

Godfrid
Count of Friezeland
(Killed 887)

Gorm the Rich
King of Northumberland
(Killed 894)

Ragnar Gormsson (d. 912)
(Latinised name – Rogerius Gormericus)
(Ancestor of the Montgomerys)

Let us now move on to the second of the Ulvungar Genealogies. This starts with Halfdan, who was King of Denmark between 810-812 AD, and whose son Anulo was killed by Olaf and his brother, Horic. Before he died Anulo had a son, Roric, who would become the founder of the Russian Royal Family. The most important of Halfdan's sons was undoubtedly Ragnar and who certainly deserved the name Ragnar Lothbroc, even if he did not kill a dragon.[6] It seems that Ragnar (or Raghnall) had under him not only the Cimbres of Seeland, but also some of the Visigoths, when he raided York in 869. From there, they appear to have gone on to raid the coasts of Spain and North Africa.[7] From Ragnar descended Guthrum, King of East Anglia, who was beaten by King Alfred and forced to accept baptism. Also from Ragnar descended Bjorn Ironside (or Bursislaw) and Sigfrid.

Sigfrid, called Frotha in the *Annals of Clonmacnois*, first appeared in history during the Danish occupation of Ireland, in the company of his brother, Awuslir (a distortion of Burislav—see later). He left Ireland, but returned with his other brother Ivar in 852, according to the *Annals of Innisfallen*. Ivar occupied Limerick, whilst Frotho or Sigfrid established himself at Waterford. His name in the *Annals* is spelt "Sitric". Later in the same year we find him moving up the Seine with his other brother, Bjorn. In 855 he sailed up the Seine as far as Perche in Champagne, but he had been wounded at the siege of Nantes and seems to have retired to Denmark. In the *Chronicles of Perche* he is called Sidroc.[8]

The conquest of East Anglia and Northumberland were left to Sigfrid's son, Gorm (or Guthrum) and his brother, Ivar Bagsaeg. Nonetheless, as the king under whom these victories took place, he is given the title by the classical writers of "Victor Anglias", and is called Anglicus I. His son, the actual leader, is called "Anclicus II"—in Danish, "hin Enske". Ivar was killed at the battle of Ashdown (Assandune) in 871.

Let us now turn to the other brother, Bjorn, known as "Ironside" (Old Swedish—Biorn Járnsiòa; Old French—Bier-Costae-Ferrae; Slavonic—Burislaw; Latin—Ursival; Irish—Awuslir). He was the lineal descendent of Herioldus Brocus and probably one of the greatest Viking kings. It is my opinion that it was he who drew up the blueprint for the re-conquest of Europe by himself and his descendents. The *Annales Bartholiniani* call him "Lothbroci Regis filius", whilst Robert Wace calls him "fiz du Lothbroc un Danois Roy". *The Three Fragments* makes it clear that Ragnar (or Raghnall) was chief of the

Aunites and that Bjorn was one of two "kings" who led the forces which destroyed York in 869, probably in revenge for Ragnar's death. Furthermore, the forces of Bjorn Ironside in France are called Visgoth/Aunites and other contemporary chronicles make Bjorn commander of the Viking raid in the Mediterranean and North Africa, which the Irish chronicles had already identified as the sons of Ragnar.[9]

Most chronicles seem to agree that Bjorn was a king in Sweden, but he must have been a Danish overlord of the region. The only contemporary king at that time with the name Bjorn was Biorn-at-Haga, who received St. Anscharius on his first visit to Birka in 829. It would seem, therefore, that they are one and the same person, famous afterwards as "Ironside".

In the Baltic island of Öland there is an enormous stronghold called Gråborg, which according to tradition was the stronghold of a king called Bugislev (or Burislaw), the Slavonic/Russian name of Bjorn Ironside. It was probably built by one of his ancestors. There is another fortified place at Ismanstorp on that same island. It is smaller and looks like a Khazak *gorodi*. On the east coast of Gotland is an enormous fortification, the Torsburgen, dating from the 5th century, the biggest of all prehistoric forts in Sweden. It covers about 264 acres and could be used as a refuge by the entire local population in time of war. These three fortifications were Bjorn's strategic strongholds in the Baltic region. From here he could control not only the Öland Sound, but also the great forests of Moere and Blekinge, which provided the wood for his fleet of war and trade ships, trading with Poland, Russia and the Baltic region.[10]

There had already been considerable trade between Scandinavia and the East even during the Bronze Age and this had not ceased, but whilst most of the ocean trade had been in the hands of the Phoenician traders, the river traffic had been in the hands of the Scandinavians. The Sviar particularly used the northern routes, the Dvina, Baltic, and the Dnieper to reach the Euxine, whilst the Volga and Caspian Sea routes used the Neva, Lake Ladoga and Wolchow. However, these routes were also raided regularly by Vikings seeking furs and slaves, particularly fair-haired women, whom they could sell in the slave markets of Bulgar and Itil or Astrakhan.[11]

Colonies were established in Novgorod, Kiev, Rostov, Smolensk and central Russia. The Khazars, a people coming from the same parts of Asia as the Cassi (or Kassi), controlled most of Southern Russia. They had intermarried with Armenians and Jews, and possibly other groupings. By the middle of the 9th century a central government was established under a Druzhina (Swedish Drott) and Bjorn was either appointed or elected to this position. It seems that the Druzhina was under the Swedish Crown, and I suppose that Bjorn was the obvious choice, as he controlled the trading routes from his southern Swedish stronghold—indeed, it may well be that this was simply Bjorn's way of consolidating his position and autonomy.

Upon Bjorn's death his enormous territory was divided between the family. Roric, his cousin, who had been a minor king in Denmark became firstly, Count of Rustringen, and later makes himself Grand Duke of Novgorod. According to Russian chronicles, Roric was a Duke in Germany and a vassal of the Roman Emperor. The only Prince who matched this is Roric, son of Anulo. As Count (but sometimes the Latin Dux is used, which can be translated as Duke) of Rustringen, he was a vassal of the Emperor. He was by all accounts a great warrior and may well have wrested the Grand Duchy from Bjorn's sons.

Of Bjorn's two sons, Helgi became Regent of Baltic Moere, Bjorn's old stronghold and later, King of Denmark, whilst Keitel (Asakeitel or Ascold) became Duke of Kiev (See Gen. II & III).

Genealogy III
Dynasty of Ulvungar
House of Lothbrook (Descent from Bjorn Ironside – See Genealogy II)

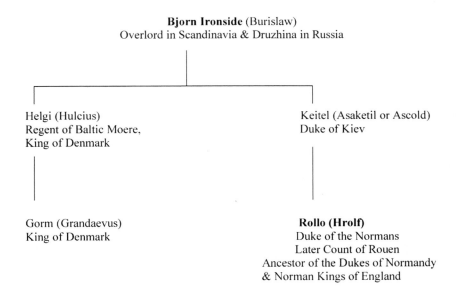

Bjorn Ironside (Burislaw)
Overlord in Scandinavia & Druzhina in Russia

Helgi (Hulcius)
Regent of Baltic Moere,
King of Denmark

Keitel (Asaketil or Ascold)
Duke of Kiev

Gorm (Grandaevus)
King of Denmark

Rollo (Hrolf)
Duke of the Normans
Later Count of Rouen
Ancestor of the Dukes of Normandy
& Norman Kings of England

This makes Rollo the third cousin once removed and slightly older of Ragnar Gormsson—see Genealogy I.

The reader will by now have noted that there was not just an eastwards expansion by the Ulvungars, but there was a clear interest in trying to wrest Western Civilisation and particularly Christian Europe from the new "Roman Empire". In modern terms they had done their marketing and were now targeting specific places. The grandsons of Raghnaill (Turgesius), King of Dublin, had established themselves firmly in Ireland. Eric and Hakon had made Norway their kingdom (Gen. I). Guthrum, now baptised and with a name change to Athelstan, was King of East Anglia and Northumberland too, had come under the sway of the Ulvungars, but the prize was undoubtedly mainland Europe and the Christian Roman Empire.

To do this, two cousins, Rollo or Hrolf and Ragnar Gormsson decide to return to France and particularly to what was to become known as Normandy. Both of their grandsires had make raids into Normandy and had established trading routes into the interior. Now they went to conquer and settle.

We will deal with the more famous Rollo, first. There is some dispute as to Rollo's ancestry and nationality at the time of his invasion of Normandy. I have dealt with this in some detail in a previous book, so will merely outline my arguments here.[12] Snorre Sturluson wrote a saga of Scandinavian kings at the beginning of the 13th century. He makes Rollo the son of the Norwegian Earl Rognvald of Moere. There is, however, no other evidence apart from Snorre's statement. Norwegians tend to support him, whilst Danes and most serious historians today, who have no particular axe to grind, tend to support the earlier chroniclers of France, Britain, Germany and Denmark. In my opinion, there is little point in these arguments as, in fact, Rollo was a native of Orkney, a so-called Hunedane and equally a native of Moere in Sweden, though the son of a Danish king.

As mentioned before, we must look for him under a variety of different names: Hrolf the Ganger, Gange-Rolf, Gange Rolf, Gange-Hrolfr, Hrolleifus, Going Rolf, Rolvo, Rolfus, Rolus, Roleff, Reolfus, Roes, Rodeo, Rodla and Rosus, to name but a few. He was also given a baptismal name on being baptised of Robert (Robertus or Rodbertus). He also had a number of Punt-names or Cognomen: Haesten and Hunedanus, to show his nationality as a Hunedane of

Orkney. On the Island of Gotland, he was known as Roes (remember Rhoes the Weoôulgeot from Gotland!) and as a native of Moere in southern Sweden, he was called Moericus.

The Norman Chronicles (*de Normanum Gestis de Francia*) are a compilation of a number of earlier chronicles: *The Annales of Eginard*, *The Annales of St. Bertin*, *The Annales of St. Waast* and other unidentified works. This work contains the following passage which refers to Rollo: "Notre dus Hastens qui Sarrazins est, et nee de Danemarche". Translated this means, "Our Duke called Hastens, who was a Viking (pirate) and was born in Denmark." This shows that Rollo was known as Hastens, he had raided the coasts of France as a Viking and was born in territory under the Danish Crown. The siege of Tours between 883-885 has been described in several chronicles. The Norman chieftain here is called Hastens or Haesten, but Monachus Floriacensis calls Rollo the leader of this expedition. All refer to the same person.

These same chronicles make it clear that, "Rollo and his band landed in Normandy on the fifteenth of the calends of December 876." Why, then, do historians think that Rollo only invaded France in 911? The above statement is too precise and is contemporary. We ignore these chronicles at our peril. Having said that, I have to confess that in a still earlier book, I also took the view that he had not landed until 911. My present research has led me to change my mind. William the Conqueror himself calls his ancestor, Hasten: "Hastinagus, antecessorum nostrum."[13]

As regards Rollo's name, Hunedanus compare these three statements:

a. The first is from *Annals Vedastine* for AD 895-896:
   "At the same time the Northmen with their Duke whose name was Hunedanus with five barges entered the Seine…the Northmen in increased numbers entered the Oise shortly before Christmas."

b. The second is from *Chron. de Gestis Normanorum de Francia* for AD 895: "The Northmen again with their Duke, who is named Rollo, entered the Seine and before Christmas day they moved up the Oise with their numbers increased."

c. The *Chron. Rerum Septrionalium* refers to the same events, but calls the leader Rodo.

Now compare these two statements:

a. The first is from *The Annales Vedastini* for the year AD 896:

"Charles (*The King of France*) raised up Huncdeus (*Hunedeus*) from the font."

b. Sigebertus Gemblaciencis refers to the same event:

"King Charles caused Hunedanus, King of the Northmen, to be baptized and raised him up from the font."

This would suggest that Rollo was baptised in 896 AD and again in 912. There are a number of possibilities here. Dr. B. G. Montgomery reckoned that Hrolf had been baptised originally in 896 and been given the baptismal name of Rollo.[14] He suggests that Rollo then returned to the religion of Odin and had to be baptised a second time in 912 AD, when he became Count of Rouen after the treaty of St. Clair-sur-Epte. He then had to be given a second "Christian" name and was now called Robert, after his new sponsor, Robert, Duke of France, the second son of Robert le fort.

This may well be true. Equally, it may simply have been an "Insurance" on the part of the French that this new noble of France should accept his "Christian" duties seriously. I mentioned also that in Gotland he was known as Roes or Rhoes, which again identifies him as a descendent of the Odonic line from Rhoes the Weoôulgeot.

There is an interesting monument in the parish of Grötlingbo on the Baltic Island of Gottland. It is called the Roes stone. It is quite small, about 33 x 22 x 3.5 inches. It depicts a hawk or bird chasing a horse. The inscription in Runic letters reads: "iudh igr r hn". We know that "iudh" is a form of Odin or Uduin and we can work out, therefore, that the bird is supposed to be the hawk of Odin. "Igr" probably is short for Iagar, which means "drives out or ejects". The "r" is generally considered to be short for Roes. Russ in Gotland means horse and Haesten is Danish for horse. The suggested meaning is that "Odin drives out Roes the horse". The question is why?

Let us suppose for a moment that Rhoes or Rollo was in fact the head of the Odonic line and chief pontiff, as I mentioned in Chapter 1. Rhoes or Roes is by way of being a title, something like The Rhoes-Haesten. Let us now suppose that Roes has been baptised and given up his Odonic beliefs. His Odonic people in Gotland would regard this as traitorous and would want to make clear that he was no longer "The Rhoes", hence that monument. "Odin drives out the Roes Haesten." It is just one more small piece in our jigsaw puzzle.

In *The Norman Families and the Conquest of England* I have gone into some detail about Rollo's parentage. Here I am merely going to summarise those findings:

a. Dudo makes clear that Rollo's father was an *Oriental Potentate*.

b. Richerus gives his name in Latin as "Catillus".

c. His name in the Saxon chronicles is Oscetil, which in Swedish would be Asakettil and in Russian Ascold.

d. The Nordic chieftain who was Duke of Kiev in 800 AD bore the name Ascold. He would have been regarded as an oriental potentate.

e. His name in the Irish chronicles is alternately Osil, Osceytil or Oscetyl. *Os* is the Gaelic for the Nordic *Asa*, a designation indicating descent from the deified kings of Norse Mythology (the Odonic Line). His full name in Swedish would have been Asakettil.

f. There was an irresistible tradition in France and England centuries before the Icelandic story-tellers appeared, that Rollo was descended from Bjorn Ironside and that his first raid on Neustria took place in 876 AD.

g. Dudo gives Rollo the Cognomen "Moericus", indicating that he was born in the hundred of Moere and that his father for a time was a petty king of that region of south Sweden.

h. Snorre has caused confusion by his statement that the sons of Harald Fair Hair, Togils and Frode, were the first Vikings to conquer Ireland. We know with certainty that Harald was not yet born, less his sons, when this deed was performed by Turges and Frotho in 838 AD.

i. Ketil Flatnose of Llandnáma belongs to the fairytales of Snorre and his group. As a contemporary of Harald's sons, he would have been seventy years younger than his supposed son-in-law; Olav the White did not marry his daughter and her name was not Aud-the-very-rich. The compilers of the Landnáma book mistook the Irish King Aodh or Aedh for a Queen, whom they called Auda. Kettil Flatnose was never king of the Isles, nor Count of the Hebrides.

Rollo was therefore a Danish Prince or possibly petty king in Southern Sweden and Gotland, the son of Asakettil (Catillus), descendent of Bjorn Ironside and Herioldus Brocus, and probably head of the cult of Odin in Gotland. There is a suggestion in some chronicles that in fact, that notwithstanding his two baptisms, he never gave up his

Odonic cult and that shortly before his death he sacrificed a hundred or more captives to Odin.

We will now examine the second and younger of the two cousins, another Ragnar—this time, Ragnar Gormsson. He was the son of Gorm the Rich, King of Northumberland, who was killed in 894 AD. According to *The Annales of St. Bertin*, in 882, Sigfrid and Gorm, his son, extorted a *Danegeld* of several thousand pounds in silver and gold. Gorm, as a consequence, became known as "hin-rikhe", which translates as "the rich". After his father's death in 887, Gorm was elected as King of Northumberland in his father's place. Presumably, he also inherited his father's part of the Danegeld. I think it likely, therefore, that he financed the invasion of Normandy by Rollo and Ragnar. Rollo would obviously have been the leader of the group, being both the elder and more experienced warrior, but at some stage during the Normandy campaign the two groups split. When I wrote *The Montgomery Millennium* [15], I had been looking at the history of the period from a purely family point of view and did not examine the various chronicles from a wider perspective. I therefore took the accepted view at the time, that Rollo had not arrived in France before 911 and that therefore the ancestor of the Montgomerys, Ragnar Gormsson (in Latin, Rogerius Gormerici), had settled in France before Rollo arrived. I now think this was wrong.

What I think happened is that Ragnar was baptised in 896, at the same time as Hrolf, and given the baptismal name of Roger. He would, however, have had his own followers and agreed to settle in Exmes. By 905 he had become Comte d'Exmes. Possibly, when his father was killed in 894, Roger decided that his future lay in France. At all events when he died in 912, he had perhaps set the tone for the future—perhaps because he had shown that Norsemen could become good Normans and, if given responsibility as Counts, could rule wisely. This may have been the catalyst for Rollo becoming Count of Rouen. It may even have been at Roger's suggestion; he was, after all, called Roger Magnus by the chroniclers. His descendent, Roger de Montgomery, was proud to call himself the son of Roger the Great, "magni Rogerii filius." [16]

These two cousins were to lay the ground, not only for the formation of the Duchy of Normandy, but for the future conquest of England and the reconquest of Aquitaine. But first let us look at their descendents. Genealogy IV shows the descendents of Hrolf, whilst Genealogy V shows the descendents of Roger the Great.

Ulvungar Dynasty
Genealogy IV
House of Normandy

From Genealogy III

Hrolf the Ganger (d/c.928)
(Rollo, Count of Rouen)

= (a) Poppa
(dau. Berenger of Bayeaux)

=(b) Gizelle
(dau. Charles, King of France)

William "Longsword" (d. 942)
= (a) Espriota
(b) Leutgarda
(dau. Herbert II of Vermandois)

Richard I (d. 995)
= (a) Emma (dau. Hugh, The Great of Paris)
(b) Gunnora of Denmark

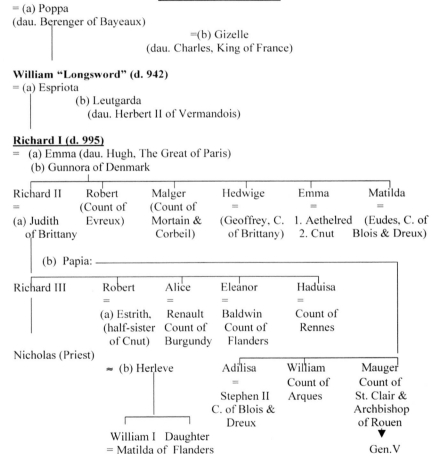

Richard II	Robert	Malger	Hedwige	Emma	Matilda
=	(Count of	(Count of	=	=	=
(a) Judith	Evreux)	Mortain &	(Geoffrey, C.	1. Aethelred	(Eudes, C. of
of Brittany		Corbeil)	of Brittany)	2. Cnut	Blois & Dreux)

(b) Papia:

Richard III	Robert	Alice	Eleanor	Haduisa
	=	=	=	=
	(a) Estrith,	Renault	Baldwin	Count of
	(half-sister	Count of	Count of	Rennes
	of Cnut)	Burgundy	Flanders	
Nicholas (Priest)				
	≈ (b) Herleve		Adilisa	William
			=	Count of
			Stephen II	Arques
			C. of Blois &	
			Dreux	

Mauger
Count of
St. Clair &
Archbishop
of Rouen
▼
Gen.V

William I   Daughter
= Matilda of Flanders

Genealogy V
Dynasty of Ulvunger
Montgomery

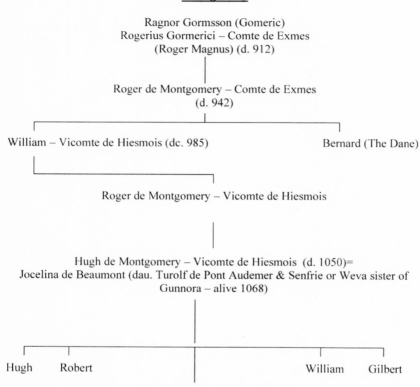

Ragnor Gormsson (Gomeric)
Rogerius Gormerici – Comte de Exmes
(Roger Magnus) (d. 912)

Roger de Montgomery – Comte de Exmes
(d. 942)

William – Vicomte de Hiesmois (dc. 985)   Bernard (The Dane)

Roger de Montgomery – Vicomte de Hiesmois

Hugh de Montgomery – Vicomte de Hiesmois (d. 1050)=
Jocelina de Beaumont (dau. Turolf de Pont Audemer & Senfrie or Weva sister of
Gunnora – alive 1068)

Hugh   Robert   William   Gilbert

Roger Comte de Montgomery (d. 1/8/1095) =
Mabel de Bellême

It was during the time of William Longsword and the second Roger
(1st to be called Montgomery, or Mons Gomerici) that the eventual
Duchy of Normandy was extended from a small enclave into a major
county, with William becoming Count of Normandy and Roger his
Viscount for lower Normandy. Curiously, they both died in 942. It was
Richard I, who first called himself "Duke", and Bernard, called the
Dane, who became his close adviser. These two again helped to forge
Normandy into a Duchy and manageable whole.[16]

The Beaumonts, another set of Norman cousins, who became
castellans of Exmes, married into the family of their Dukes and Hugh

de Montgomery continued to renew their interrelationship by, in turn, marrying Joscelina de Beaumont.

I have dealt at length with the various inter-marriages between this small group of Norman families, which resulted in the Conquest of England, in my book *The Norman Families and the Conquest of England*, so I will merely give a synopsis of the positions of each in that momentous undertaking.

William's staff and Inner Circle consisted of the following:

Robert de Beaumont—became Head of the Regency Council together with the Duchess Matilda and Hugh d'Avranches.

Robert d'Eu—was in charge of the advanced camp at Saint-Valery.

William FitzOsbern—was in charge of logistics once they reached England.

Roger de Montgomery—was in charge of logistics and strategy at the assembly point in Dives.

At the battle of Hastings:

William was in charge of the Centre, together with his half-brothers, Odo of Bayeaux, and the Count of Mortain.

Roger de Montgomery and Eustace of Boulogne were in charge of the Right Wing. Alan of Brittany and Aimeri de Thouars were in charge of the Left Wing.

All were close cousins.

The Ulvungar Dynasty was back in England and had achieved a large slice of their grand dream. They controlled a large chunk of Northern France and now all of England. William is king, but Roger de Montgomery and other close cousins were made Earls Palatine—effectively kings in their own areas. Roger's ancestor Gorm had been King of Northumberland; Roger got Shropshire, parts of Staffordshire, Pembroke, Kendal, Lancaster and parts of North Wales and Anglesey, plus the rape of Arundel. In Normandy he was already Count of Montgomery, Bellême, de Say & Alençon. Others of the family benefited just as much.

Chapter 7 References

1. "Olaf Kunung Rings bane, Goder son" – *Series Runica Prima*. Courtesy of the Danish State Archives.

2. Lair, J. (1885) – *Introductory Notes to Dudon de Saint-Quention*, Mémoires de la Société de Antiquitaires de Normandie.

3. For a complete analysis see Montgomery, H. (2004) – *The Norman Families and the Conquest of England*, App. I-VI; Also Crouch, D. (2002) – *The Normans, The History of a Dynasty*, p. 4 & Table 1, Hambledon & London, London, UK; Worsac, J. (1863) – *Den danske Erobring af England og Normanniet*; Steenstrup, J. (1882) – *Normannerne*; Wahlberg, E. – (1913) *Sur l'Origine de Rollon*; Revel, J. (1918) – *Historie des Normans*; de Montgomery, B. G. (1968) – *Ancient Migrations and Royal Houses*, Chap. 11, Mitre Press, London.

4. *The Three Fragments* – A manuscript preserved in the Burgundian Library in Brussels. It contains, amongst other pieces, the genealogy of King Ingvar of Dublin (872 AD). These are also included in *Annals of the Kingdom of Ireland by the Four Masters*, ed. & trans. by O'Donovan, J. (1887-1901), 7 vols. Dublin.

5. Letter from Bernt Klafstad, Finstad, Norway, dated 22nd Jan., 2004.

6. Cornelius Hamsfort (1546-1627) was the owner of the most important collection of ancient documents relating to Danish History, the *Regum Danorum* series. He states that Ragnar succeeded his brother Harold as King of the Cimbri of Seeland. It appears, therefore, that Ragnar was overlord of the Cimbric population in central Jutland, the Danish Isles and the South of Sweden.

7. *The Three Fragments* – contains the following: "At this time (869) the Aunites (i.e. *The Danes*) came with countless forces to Caer Ebroic (*York*), and destroyed the city, which they took…(*then they rowed*) forward across the Cantabrian Sea, the sea that is between Erin and Spain…and they were guilty of many outrages in Spain…. They afterwards crossed the Gaditanean Straits…and arrived in Africa; where they fought a battle with the Mauretani, in which great slaughter of the Mauretani was made." (my italics)

8. *Chron. Fontaneille* in the Library in Perche.

9. Wace, R. (c.1135) – *Le Roman de Rou* – ed. A. J.Holden, 3 vols.;

Soc.des anciens texts français (1970-73). Also, *The Three Fragments*; Also, *Fraga. Mirac. S. Bercharii*.

10. Montgomery, H. (2004) – *The Norman Families op. cit.* App. XX-XXI; Also, de Montgomery, B. G. *op. cit.* Chap. 13.

11. Clough, S. B. & Cole, C. W. (1967) – *Economic History of Europe*, Chap. III, Heath and Company, Boston.

12. See note 10; also Crouch, D., *op. cit.*

13. William of Malmesbury (c. 1120) – *De gestis regum Anglorum*.

14. de Montgomery, B. G. *op. cit.* p. 143; see also Montgomery, H. *op. cit.* App. X.

15. Montgomery, H. (2002) – *The Montgomery Millennium*, p. v. Megatrend, London & Belgrade.

16. Montgomery, *The Norman Families, op. cit.* App. XXIX (quoting Cartulary of Troarn, folio 1).

17. For a complete history of this period see Crouch, D. *op. cit.* Chaps. 1 & 2. Also Montgomery, B. G. (1948) – *Origin and History of the Montgomerys*, Blackwood, Edinburgh & London. Also, Montgomery, H., *Montgomery Millennium, op. cit.* p. v-x & 1-5. Also Montgomery, H., *The Norman Families, op. cit.* Chap. II. Also, Brown, R.A. (1984) – *The Normans*, Chaps. 1-3, Boydell Press, London.

Chapter 8

The Ulvungar and Exilarch Lines

In Chapter 7 I showed that the Exilarch line had continued well into the Medieval period via the Kalonymos line of the Hassidim, but there was also a line via the House of Charlemagne. Whether or not the line remained at heart Jewish, I cannot say, but what is clear is that the lines were certainly well disposed towards their Jewish heritage.

After the Conquest of England many Jews moved over. Some were undoubtedly merchants, but equally many were landowners. The Norman kings called the Jews "His Jews", meaning the king's Jews.[1] The Norman kings gave the Jews special rights and granted them a series of Charters, one of which, issued in 1201, says that they are permitted to reside in the king's lands (Allodial land kept by the king and registered in Domesday). Furthermore, they were to travel where they would and to have secure possession of their "lands, fiefs, pledges and escheats (reverted estates)". This shows clearly that there must have been major Jewish landholders in England after the conquest and as King William I had given the land out in the first place, one must presume that he granted some Jews considerable land.

Their rights went even further. In Law a Jew need only appear before the Royal Judges (in practice, the king himself). In a case between a Christian and a Jew, the plaintiff, whether Jew or Christian, had to have a witness of both religions (cases were principally settled by the swearing of witnesses). In the absence of witnesses, a Jew could clear himself by an oath on the Roll of the Law (Torah). Even more importantly, when a Christian brought a case against a Jew, unless it was the Crown, the case was "to be judged by the Jew's fellows". The only other group with similar rights were members of the Peerage. Effectively, William and his descendents are saying, *Jews have the rank of Nobles*. It went even further—their rights in chattels and debts were *guaranteed* and they were free from tolls and customs.[2]

Jewish Ritual Bath (courtesy of David Derbyshire of the Daily Telegraph)

In 2003 a mikvah or ritual bath was excavated under Milk Street in the city of London (see photograph). This bath has been dated to approximately 1066. It is within the agreed walking distance for a Jewish woman to go for her ritual ablution from the White Tower. Is this coincidence? I think not. I think that there were Jews in high positions within William's Court living in the White Tower, the first part of the Tower of London to be built by William to guard London. Another ritual bath was built slightly later in Bristol.

When William II came to the throne and his brother, Robert of Normandy, needed funds to go on the Crusade, it was the Jews who lent William the money to give to his brother in return for a mortgage on Normandy. It was beginning to look as if the early Norman kings were doing exactly the same as Charlemagne had done just over two hundred years before, except that William was a king and not an emperor. It was looking as if some of William's family were very much interested in promoting Judaism. The question was why? Okay, the dynasty was descended from Ataulf and Maria, but was there a more recent marriage?

If my suspicions were correct then there would have had to have been a marriage into the Davidic line somewhere. The obvious place to look was at William the Conqueror's family and ancestry. Apart from those in the direct line from Rollo, there were other collateral branches, many of whom took the name Saint Clair, presumably from the treaty place of St. Clair-sur-Epte. In Latin the surname was normally Sancto Claro and over the years in Britain was usually spelt as Sinclair, though a number of variations exist. For example in Somerton, Somerset, the name is St. Cleer and in Sweden, Sinklar. However, surnames were still not used much and most landowners were known by their territorial names.

I started with William's known ancestors and immediate family. If you look at Genealogy IV, you will see that there were a number of possibilities. The first obvious person was Gizelle, daughter of King Charles the Simple. Charles's father had been Charles the Bald and his mother, Richild, daughter of Count Buwin of Autun. His grandfather had been Louis the Debonair (later called the Pious) and his grandmother had been Judith, daughter of the first Makhir of Septimania. Count Buwin too, is likely to have been connected to the Septimanian family. The problem was that none of the children of Hrolf and Gizelle survived infancy and his son, William Longsword, was by his mistress

Poppa, though it was possible that they had gone through some sort of Viking ceremony (*more Danico,* according to William of Jumièges). So who was Poppa? The truth is, we don't know. There is a chronicle that links her to Count Berenger of Bayeaux[3], but I am not totally convinced that it can be relied upon. Indeed, I wondered if Dudo had made a mistake and that she was the daughter of Berenguer of Catalonia, which as we shall see later would make more sense.

It was possible that Gizelle had influenced Hrolf, but nothing could be proved on its own. The next person to look at was the son of Hrolf, William Longsword. He had married Leutgarda (or Liutgard), daughter of Herbert II of Vermandois, whose great-great-grandfather had been Pepin, son of Charlemagne. Once again, no children survived, but after William's death Leutgarda married Theobald, Count of Blois and Chartres. This might bear looking into later. William Longsword's long-term companion, however, was Espriota (or Sprota), who, apart from the fact that she was Breton, was otherwise a complete blank.

Next on my list was Richard I. Again, he had originally married Emma, daughter of Hugh the Great, of Paris and Dux Francorum and his third wife, Hadwig, sister of Otto I, but once again they had had no issue. Richard II's second wife had been Gunnora of Denmark. Prof. Crouch, in his book *The Normans*, makes the point that Gunnora had started off being a concubine and had later married Richard and that by doing so, Richard allied himself with another royal Danish dynasty, who might otherwise prove a rival to him. Gunnora's family were large landowners in western Normandy and she was wealthy in her own right. So who were her family? According to a document I came across in the Danish archives, she and her sisters descended from Harold Bluetooth, King of Denmark. Whether this is true I do not know, but her family were certainly a very important dynasty, so it may well be true and could indeed prove a rival to Richard. We do know that she had a brother, Arfast, whose descendents were the family of FitzOsbern, mentioned in Chapter 7, as one of William's cousins. Interestingly, by 1110 at least seven of the great Counts and Earls of the Anglo-Norman aristocracy, including Henry I himself, were directly descended from Gunnora and her sisters. But none of this was helping with my question as to why the Jews were given such extraordinary rights under the Norman and Angevin kings.

I went through each of the marriages and liaisons in turn—Judith of Brittany and Papia, respectively wife and mistress of Richard II, until

I came to William's mother. Herleve was the mistress of Robert, Duke of Normandy, and mother of William. She was not the daughter of a tanner, as some historians still quote from the Anglo-Saxon chronicle, but the daughter of Fulbert. Fulbert had the title of "Cubicularius", something equivalent to the court chamberlain in the household of Duke Robert. It was undoubtedly in those circumstances that Robert and Herleve met.[4] Now that is just the sort of position in which many high ranking Jews were used. They were considered more trustworthy than one's own family, who might wish to get rid of a rival. After all, Robert had almost certainly poisoned his brother Richard to obtain the dukedom, so he, of all people, would want as a chamberlain somebody he could trust not to poison him.

Bernard of Septimania had been appointed to the same job for the Emperor Louis and been guardian of the infant Charles. The Count of Flanders had appointed Herleve to be the guardian of his daughter. William had furthermore been brought up in his mother's household until Robert proclaimed him his heir, so if she had been either openly or secretly a Jewess, he would have learnt respect for her people from her.

Was there any proof of this? I could not find any direct proof, but there was a curious piece of circumstantial evidence.

In 1051 William had been busy fighting Geoffrey Martel and had laid siege to Domfront. He then left Roger de Montgomery in charge and made a dash for Alençon, catching the town unawares and nearly galloping his cavalry into the town.

The townspeople, thinking that their walls were impregnable, hung hides over the walls and taunted him, calling, "Hides! Hides for the Tanner!" It is from this that the idea that Herleve's father was a tanner, derives. The point was that at that time many of the Jewish artisan class were in fact tanners, according to Israel Abrahams in his book *Jewish Life in the Middle Ages*. I went on a research trip to Alençon when I was researching another book and, although I was unable to find any lists for the year 1051, there were list for about 150 years later. The names are quite clear—Samuel, Isaac and other Jewish names occur as tanners. As these trades were generally inherited, it is not unlikely that the tanners in Alençon were Jews in 1051 and that knowing his mother to be Jewish, what the townsmen were doing was saying the equivalent of, "Hey! Jewboy come and get us!"

The story is that the town was taken because the gates were opened during the night and William's troops were able to get in without the town's people being aware and that the main gates were then opened for William's troops to charge in. Who opened them? There are two theories. The first is that some of William's soldiers actually managed to get in, in that first mad rush unknown to the townsmen, and then hid and opened the gates. The second is that sympathisers in the town let in William's troops. If the latter is true then perhaps the sympathisers were co-religionists of William's mother. They had done this, after all, for Pepin at Narbonne!

William exacted a terrible revenge for the insult to his mother. He had thirty-two of the leading citizens paraded in front of the townspeople and had their hands and feet cut off. William then threatened the castle's garrison with the same fate if they did not surrender immediately. Somewhat naturally they surrendered on the spot. Okay, this was not proof, but it was a likely probability. I now needed to look at his other relatives and see what this might bring.

I started with another Charlemagnic line of descent, which was well known—those of the Counts of Ponthieu and the Counts of Boulogne (see Descent from Charlemagne genealogy chart in Chap. 6). Ericule, the son of William of Ponthieu, became Count of Boulogne but his direct male line finished when his two sons, Eustache and Arnoul, predeceased their father. The line continued via his daughter Mahout (a curious form of Maud used in the grail saga *Titurel*, by Wolfram von Eschenbach), who married Adolphe, Count of Guines, and their son in turn became Count of Boulogne. The name Mahout is interesting in that it is not a French name, but distinctly Arabic or Hebrew in origin. For example in Arabic, *Maut* means a dead body and in Hebrew, *Mahalut* suggests remembering the dead.[5] It seems likely that Mahout was a name given to remember their past and therefore, that at least up until Ericule, their Semitic ancestry was remembered. I could now go one step further and trace the descent from Eustace, the great-grandson of Mahout.[6]

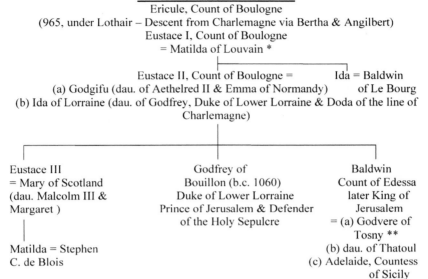

COMMON DESCENT FROM
Ericule, Count of Boulogne
(965, under Lothair – Descent from Charlemagne via Bertha & Angilbert)
Eustace I, Count of Boulogne
= Matilda of Louvain *

Eustace II, Count of Boulogne =   Ida = Baldwin
(a) Godgifu (dau. of Aethelred II & Emma of Normandy)   of Le Bourg
(b) Ida of Lorraine (dau. of Godfrey, Duke of Lower Lorraine & Doda of the line of
Charlemagne)

Eustace III	Godfrey of	Baldwin
= Mary of Scotland	Bouillon (b.c. 1060)	Count of Edessa
(dau. Malcolm III &	Duke of Lower Lorraine	later King of
Margaret)	Prince of Jerusalem & Defender	Jerusalem
	of the Holy Sepulcre	= (a) Godvere of
		Tosny **
Matilda = Stephen		(b) dau. of Thatoul
C. de Blois		(c) Adelaide, Countess
		of Sicily

* Adela of Louvain was the 1st wife of Henry I of England. His 2nd. wife was
Matilda, sister of Mary of Scotland.
**William FitzOsborn, cousin of William the Conqueror, had married Aeliz de Tosny
(her Aunt ?).

This pedigree immediately threw up a number of interesting relationships. Eustace II married into the Ulvungar dynasty of Normandy and a remarriage back into the Davidic line from Charlemagne. More interesting still was that his son, Godfrey, became Prince of Jerusalem and Defender of the Holy Sepulchre, the same title as Charlemagne's. When Godfrey died his brother Baldwin became King of Jerusalem. He had, in fact, regained his inheritance as King of Judea. What is more, as King of Jerusalem he took precedence over all European monarchs. The Davidic line had returned to their roots. It was also obvious that the intermarriages with the Norman Ulvungar dynasty were striking—Tosny, FitzOsbern and Henry, King of England and later also, Duke of Normandy. But there was also another family that needed to be considered if I was to prove my point—the Montgomerys.

Genealogy V in Chapter 7 shows the marriage between Roger de Montgomery and Mabile of Bellême. Mabile has been given very bad press by the Clergy—"Daughter of Satan", being amongst the worst. She had been accused of being a poisoner, but the thing that really got up the noses of the priests was that during Roger's absence in England she donned armour and led her troops into battle against some rebels.

Whilst doing some research on my family's history, my wife and I spent a couple of weeks in Normandy researching local archival material. I went to the local Marie to see if I could look at their records, but was told by the receptionist that the archives were closed for the summer holidays. It was September. Luckily, I speak reasonable French and pointed out gently that my name was Montgomery and that I was a direct lineal descendent of Robert of Bellême. There was an immediate change of attitude. The Mayor was consulted and I was handed the key to their Library, where the records were kept, with the request to hand it in to reception when I had finished.

My wife and I then spent a day delving into local records with the result that I was able to draw up the following pedigrees:

1. Descent from the Merovignians[7]

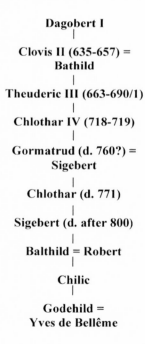

Dagobert I
|
Clovis II (635-657) =
Bathild
|
Theuderic III (663-690/1)
|
Chlothar IV (718-719)
|
Gormatrud (d. 760?) =
Sigebert
|
Chlothar (d. 771)
|
Sigebert (d. after 800)
|
Balthild = Robert
|
Chilic
|
Godehild =
Yves de Bellême

2. Descent from Yves de Bellême [8]

Yves de Bellême (d. 940)
Grand Master of Crossbowmen
Governor of Creil
= Godehilde (d. after 1005)
(4 x great grand daughter of Chlothar IV)

Guilluime I (1005 - 1031)
Seigneur of Alençon and Prince of Bellême
(Confidant of Robert the Pious)
= Mathilde

Robert I de Bellême
(1031 - 1033)
(Killed Chateau de Ballon)

Guilluime II de Talvas (or Talvais)
(1033 - 1053)
"Prince of Belleme"
=(a) Hildeburge
=(b) Daughter of Raoul de Beaumont

Mabile (Daughter of Guilluime II)
(1053 - 1082)
(Killed Chateau de Bures-sur-Dives)
= Roger de Montgomery
Vicomte d'Exmes (Hiesmois)

Robert II de Montgomery (Talvas)
(1082 - 1114)
Prince of Bellême
(Was dispossessed of Bellême by Henry I and died in prison after 1127)
= Agnes de Ponthieu

(There are some differences in dates regarding the death of Robert II de Bellême. The dates in brackets are the dates of titular possession.)

There were some immediately obvious points. The first was that Mabile descended from a line of Merovignian kings. Both her father and her son held the title of "Prince". The second was why was she so hated by the Church? In my earlier book, *Montgomery Millennium*, I had postulated that Mabile had either been a practicing Jewess or an Elchasaite. One thing was clear, she did not bother attending Mass except about once a year and I suspect that was just for show. Du Motey gives this portrait of her: "She was a young girl, quite small, with an exceptional 'finesse d'esprit' and full of energy. She was cheerful, expressed herself with great ease and made her decisions boldly." It is Ordericus Vitalis who says she was "cruel and inclined to do evil".[9]   Her husband, Roger, however, endowed the Church of Troarn and made provision for twelve Monks.

Yuri and I examined all that we could find out about her. Family documents tend to make out that she was pious, but we quickly came to the conclusion that this was to try and overcome the Church's propaganda and based upon a belief that she must have been a Christian. Our tentative hypothesis was that she was a member of the Elchasaites. Our problem was that there was no apparent reason for this, as the Merovingian dynasty did not descend from the marriage of Ataulf with Maria of the Elchasaites. There was another dynastic marriage, however, that could have brought the Elchasaic ideas into the Talvas family and that was the marriage of Sigismund's daughter, Suavegotha, to Thierry or Theodoric I, particularly as her mother, Sigismund's second wife, had been Ostragotha. This, however, implied that there was a female line of knowledge, which cascaded down the centuries. For the moment I left it there and went on to look for a marriage into the Exilarch line of the Makhirs. Sure enough, there it was! Robert de Bellême had married Agnes of Ponthieu, direct descendent of Charlemagne's daughter Bertha, with Angilbert. We therefore had a position of Robert's mother, Mabile, as being a possible follower of Elchasai and his wife being a descendent of the Makhirs of Septimania, a powerful combination—particularly as he, himself, was a descendent of the Davidic and Odonic lines, as was his cousin, King William I.

This was made even more obvious if one looked at the Ponthieu line and saw that Robert of Bellême's son William had married the daughter of the Duke of Burgundy. She just happened to be the widow of Bertrand of Toulouse, the very centre of the old Septimanian Princedom, and later the family that would protect the Cathars. It looked as though I was right. It also put these bloodlines into the family of Steward, who were to become the kings of a United Kingdom of Britain.

PONTHIEU LINE FROM CHARLEMAGNE

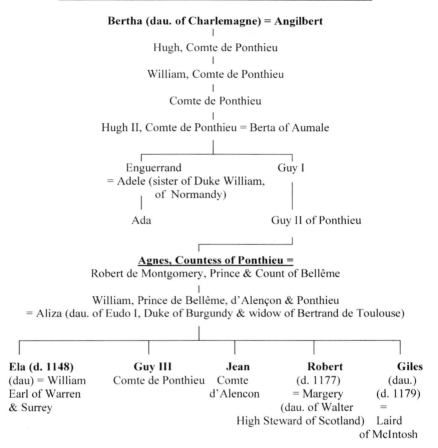

Bertha (dau. of Charlemagne) = Angilbert

Hugh, Comte de Ponthieu

William, Comte de Ponthieu

Comte de Ponthieu

Hugh II, Comte de Ponthieu = Berta of Aumale

Enguerrand
= Adele (sister of Duke William,
of Normandy)

Ada

Guy I

Guy II of Ponthieu

Agnes, Countess of Ponthieu =
Robert de Montgomery, Prince & Count of Bellême

William, Prince de Bellême, d'Alençon & Ponthieu
= Aliza (dau. of Eudo I, Duke of Burgundy & widow of Bertrand de Toulouse)

Ela (d. 1148)	**Guy III**	**Jean**	**Robert**	**Giles**
(dau) = William	Comte de Ponthieu	Comte	(d. 1177)	(dau.)
Earl of Warren		d'Alencon	= Margery	(d. 1179)
& Surrey			(dau. of Walter	=
			High Steward of Scotland)	Laird
				of McIntosh

One thing more was required. The St. Clairs, William the Conqueror's cousins, needed to marry into this line. I mentioned earlier that many of the St. Clairs were better known by their territorial titles and one such was Robert Fitz-Hamon de St. Clair, Seigneur and later Count of Corbeil. He had married Sibil, daughter of Roger de Montgomery and sister of Robert de Bellême. What is more, their grand-daughter, Melisende, married Hugh I of Rethel, son of Baldwin of Le Bourg, Count of Rethel and cousin to Godfrey and Baldwin, King of Jerusalem. Someone once said, "Once is an accident, twice is a coincidence, three times is enemy action." In this case, we had to be looking at a deliberate policy to maintain these bloodlines.

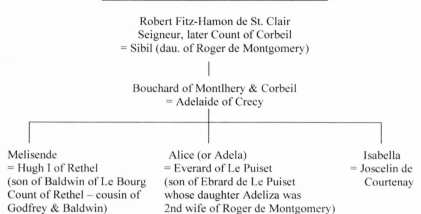

COMMON DESCENT FROM HROLF (10)

Robert Fitz-Hamon de St. Clair
Seigneur, later Count of Corbeil
= Sibil (dau. of Roger de Montgomery)

Bouchard of Montlhery & Corbeil
= Adelaide of Crecy

Melisende	Alice (or Adela)	Isabella
= Hugh I of Rethel	= Everard of Le Puiset	= Joscelin de
(son of Baldwin of Le Bourg	(son of Ebrard de Le Puiset	Courtenay
Count of Rethel – cousin of	whose daughter Adeliza was	
Godfrey & Baldwin)	2nd wife of Roger de Montgomery)	

We now had clearly an ongoing line that encompassed not only the Odonic/Ulvungar Dynasty, but also the Davidic and Benjamite Dynasties via the Elchasaites, and the Davidic Dynasty via the Makhirs of Septimania. But the Ulvungar Dynasty of William and his cousins had not been the only Danish Dynasty with their eye on conquest.

Chapter 8 References:

1. Bartlett, R. (2000) – *England under the Norman and Angevin Kings 1075-1225*, p. 351, Clarendon Press, Oxford.

2. Montgomery, H. – *The Norman Families op. cit.* Appendix 1.

3. Dudo of St. Quentin (c. 1025) – *De moribus et actis primorum Normanniae Ducum*, ed. J. Lair, (1865), Caen.

4. McLynn, F. (1998) – *1066, The Year of the Three Battles*, p. 23, Jonathon Cape, London.

5. Eisenman, R. & Wise, M. (1992) – *The Dead Sea Scrolls Uncovered*, Fragments 1 & 2, p. 25-27, Penguin Books, London. There is also a reference to the Nasi as leader.

6. Platts, B. (1985) – *Scottish Hazard* Vol. I p. 226, Procter Press, London.

7. Mckitterick, R. op. cit. p. 350-351; Montgomery, H. *Montgomery Millennium, op. cit.* App. III-5.

8. *Chahiers Percherons*, Triem. No. 51, 3rd Trimestre, 1976. Published by Assoc. de Amis du Perche. Library of Marie de Bellême.

9. Ordericus Vitalis, *Origine de la Normandie*, p. 219, Paris Edition, (1920).

10. I am grateful to Major Niven Sinclair, Chairman of the Sinclair Trust for access to the Sinclair Charter Chest. Papal authority had to be obtained, because the marriage was between close cousins. There exists a letter from the Bishop of Sees setting out the relationships of the various members of the Montgomery Family and that of the Corbeils.

Chapter 9

Harald Hardrada and the Byzantines

Harald Hardrada was born Harald Sigurdsson. He was born circa 1015, and it is generally thought that the Viking raids, which started some two hundred years before this date, were the result of demographic pressures[1] in terms of land and population growth. It has even been suggested that polygamy was responsible for these pressures. I have to say that I disagree. Scandinavia was undergoing a periodic increase in temperature (global warming) and was considerably warmer than it was later to become. It seems that Scandinavia was able to support a considerable population though scholars disagree as to nature and size. Norway in particular seems to have been able to support a population in excess of two million by the eleventh century. There was farming of cereals such as wheat, barley, oats and rye as well as a well-established dairy farming industry and large herds of cattle. Besides this there were vast herds of elk, reindeer and red deer and enormous flocks of migratory birds such as geese and ducks. There was also abundant fishing along Norway's North Sea coast.

It seems strange, therefore, that there should have been demographic pressure. We must, however, look at how land was distributed to understand the picture fully.

The Aristocracy in Norway was comprised initially of warrior chieftains who headed a Clan on much the same basis as the Highland Chiefs in Scotland. By the beginning of the eleventh century most aristocrats were also traders. Just as Bjorn Ironside from Sweden had controlled a trading empire, so Norway's magnates held what amounted to vast trading franchises. One controlled the fur trade with England, whilst another held the franchise for trade with Finland.

Over a century before Harald's birth the kings of Norway starting with Harald Fairhair had changed the nature of land holding. Before Fairhair certain classes of nobles, the Odelsbondermen, had held their property freehold on behalf of the family or clan, who had the absolute right to redeem any property sold outside the immediate family. Harald Fairhair changed this and made landholding not only provisional, but he did not give the magnates even the rights enjoyed under feudalism — that of prerogatives over sub vassals inherent in feudalism. He effectively abolished the system of Clan ownership and just as this resulted in the clearances in Scotland in a later century and mass emigration to the States, so in the tenth century many Norwegian nobles and their clans, also looked elsewhere[2].

There was another reason for leaving as well. Sometime before 1000 AD, the Norwegian king, Olaf Tryggvason, converted to Christianity. There was considerable opposition from the Odonic line and their followers and in the year 1000 AD, Olaf Tryggvason was defeated and killed by an alliance of Ulvungars, led by the kings of Sweden and Denmark and, in particular, Gorm's grandson, Sven Forkbeard[3], later king of England, who raised Olaf's own nobles against him. Norway was now divided between Denmark and Sweden, with the Jarls Erik and Sven ruling the country as vassals to the Ulvungars.

During the next sixteen years Norway reverted to what it had been, with petty kings ruling independent districts. One such was Sigurd Syr, who ruled over the areas of Hadeland and Toten; another was the great-grandson of Harald Fairhair, called Harald Grenske. About 990 Harald Grenske married Aasta. In 993 a boy, Olaf, was born but his father died before his birth. Aasta then married Sigurd Syr, who brought up Olaf as his own son. During Olaf Tyggvason's reign, he insisted that the boy, Olaf Haraldsson, be baptised with his name. I assume he stood as Godfather. Olaf Haraldsson, notwithstanding his baptism, joined various Viking expeditions to Denmark and Sweden and eventually finished up in England where he lived until 1013. He spent a further two years in Normandy and in 1015 returned to Norway with a large force determined to try and regain the throne of his ancestor, Harald Fairhair, and Christianise the country.

He was backed by Sigurd Syr, who persuaded a number of other petty kings to support Olaf. By 1016 Olaf was strong enough to meet Jarl Sven in battle. At Nesjar, Olaf beat Sven decisively and Olaf was proclaimed King of Norway. By 1019 he had started his forced Christianisation programme, by blinding and maiming those who would not desert their old Gods. Odinism was driven underground and those who did accept Christianity did so by overlaying one religion with another. Odin, as the story goes, had hung on a tree to obtain wisdom, while Jesus had hung on a cross. Jesus was given both the powers of Odin and Thor whilst Freya became the Virgin Mary.

The old aristocracy bided its time. In 1028 Olaf Haraldsson and the new king of Sweden decided to attack Denmark, whilst they thought Cnut was busy with his new kingdom of England. Cnut immediately was informed, assembled a fleet and returned to Norway. He was joined there by the disgruntled aristocracy, who proceeded to proclaim Cnut, King of Norway. Olaf fled first to Sweden and then to join Grand Duke Yaroslav in Kiev. One must be a little careful of all this information, which comes principally from the Olaf Sagas of Snorre Sturlusson, but it can be confirmed elsewhere—in this case, from Ordo Niderosiensis Ecclesiae.[4]

Olaf tried to make a comeback in 1030. He recruited some Varangian guards from Constantinople and raised more forces in Sweden. Amongst those who joined him was his own half-brother, Harald Sigurdsson, now about 15. In the ensuing battle Olaf's forces were outnumbered by about two to one.[5] Olaf was slain and most of his forces as well. Harald Sigurdsson was badly wounded and would probably have died if it had not been for a certain Rognvald Bruisson, who rescued Harald and found a peasant family to nurse him and tend his wounds.

Once his wounds were healed Harald headed for Sweden, hiding by day and moving by night. Harald stayed in Sweden until 1031, when he travelled to Kiev. This was a place to which many exiled Scandinavians came. Its Prince, Yaroslav, had been Grand Duke of Novgorod and had come to power with the aid of Scandinavian warriors.

Olaf, Harald's half-brother, was well known in Kiev, having lived there in 1029. Harald himself was welcomed warmly. According to the Sagas, Harald fought in Yaroslav's armies alongside his companion, Eilif, son of Rognvald of Orkney. The problem, as I have pointed out elsewhere, is that there is not proof of Rognvald's existence outside of the Sagas, so I am very cautious about this period of Harald's life. The story is that he asked for the hand of Elizabeth, Yaroslav's daughter, when she came of age. Frankly, I doubt this. What is clear is that in 1034 Harald left the employ of Yaroslav and sailed for Byzantium. I think it possible that Yaroslav had already an eye on a conquest of Byzantium, and made an offer to Harald that he would reward him well if Harald sent back information to Yaroslav about Byzantium's defences. Perhaps Yaroslav hinted at a marriage into his family at some future date.

Harald had little difficulty in enrolling into the elite Varangian Guard, which had become a major component of the Byzantine Army, under the Emperor Basil II.

By the time that Harald joined them, the Varangians had acquired very considerable expertise. They were equally adept at fighting on horseback or on foot. They knew how to throw up temporary fortifications, employing both stakes and ditches, just as the old Roman Legions had done. They could also wage guerrilla warfare and were the medieval equivalent of the S.A.S. It was also during this period that Basil II started training an elite within an elite, The Varangian Bodyguard, as opposed to the Varangian Mercenary Guards.

Harald started life in the Mercenary Guard as did all new recruits. It is difficult to ascertain with accuracy Harald's early service, but it is likely that he took part in several naval engagements against one or another set of pirates.

We do know that Harald took part in the Byzantine campaign in Southern Italy and in particular Sicily between 1038-1041. This campaign is particularly well documented from both European and Arab sources. At that time Italy was divided into a number of regions. In the South, Calabria (The Toe of Italy) and Apulia (The Heel of Italy) were part of the Byzantine Empire, with its local administrative centre at Bari. The Western Roman Emperors, as heir of Charlemagne, and now, kings of Germany, claimed suzerainty over all of Lombardy and Italy, but the papacy also claimed the whole of Italy under the mythical "Donation of Constantine". They had, however, a real claim from Charlemagne, who had granted them Spoleto or Benevento and most of Southern Italy. Sicily belonged to Islam since the mid 800's. On the ground the local Lombard principalities of Capua, Salerno and Benevento were virtually independent and on the West Coast the four Duchies of Amalfi, Sorrento, Naples and Gaeta were quasi-autonomous, but attached politically to the Byzantine "Catapanate of Italy". There was also the great Benedictine Abbey and Monastery of Montecassino, which was a separate principality (Terra Sancti Benedicti).[6]

In Sicily, two Arab chieftains battled for supremacy. One of them Akhal Aboulafar, asked the Byzantine Emperor for aid, whilst the other, Abou Hafs, asked the Caliph in Tunis for military help. The new

Emperor, Michael IV, sent the Catapan of Italy, Constantine Opus, to help Akhal, whilst the Caliph sent his son, Abdallah-ibn-Muizz, to reinforce Abou. The campaign did not go well for the Byzantines and Opus was forced to retire from Sicily. Michael IV then put together a huge army that included the Varangians, Normans under the Hauteville brothers, as well as levies from the Byzantine Catapanate from Apulia and Calabria. All of these troops were placed under the command of Georgios Maniakes, who was the most famous commander of his time.

Maniakes was as big as Harald and with a far greater reputation. He and Harald appear to have disliked each other on sight. Harald was at this time in command of some five hundred Varangians and, if you believe the Sagas, it was always Harald and his Varangians who made the breaches and beachheads and it was Maniakes who always threw away his chances. Certainly Maniakes must bear considerable responsibility for the disastrous campaign. In fact, Maniakes's army fell apart, with the Normans and Varangians openly opposing Maniakes. The aftermath of the victory at Traina was a disaster. Harald and his Varangians were recalled to Constantinople to help subdue the Bulgarians, who had risen in revolt against Byzantium. The Lombards and Normans then rose against Maniakes and proceeded to inflict crushing defeat after crushing defeat on the remaining Byzantine forces including the remaining Varangians, many of whom were drowned in the river Ofanto, which was in full flood.

Meanwhile, Harald made his mark at Thessalonica. He and his men distinguished themselves to such an extent that Harald was awarded the title of Manglavites and the rank of Spatharocandidatus. Unfortunately, shortly after this Michael IV died and was replaced by a somewhat unsavoury character, the son of a dockworker, who reigned as Michael V. He, on the advice of Maniakes, disbanded the Varangian Guard and replaced them with Scythians. Harald was thrown into prison on charges, some of which were valid and some of which were trumped up. Michael then turned on the Empress Zoe and had her arrested, however he had misread the people's love for Zoe and the crowd turned on his guards and proceeded to attack the Imperial Palace. There, they were joined by the Varangians, thirsting for revenge for their humiliation by Michael and Maniakes. Harald was released from prison. His titles and rank were restored to him and the Varangians were reinstalled as Guards. They were now ordered to capture Michael and his co-sponsor, Constantine, and to blind them both. When they arrived at the Studite Monastery where the ex-Emperor had taken refuge, they found that the mob was there before them. The mob happily handed Michael and Constantine over to Harald, having already dragged the two from the sanctuary of the altar. Harald now proceeded to carry out his orders, blinding both the ex-Emperor and his sponsor. Harald was appointed senior commander of the Varangians. He had amassed a vast treasure and already was building up a group of loyal followers within members of the guard.

Harald now decided that the time had come to leave Constantinople. Various arguments have been advanced as to why he decided at this time. My own opinion is that there were various reasons. His old enemy, Maniakes, had had himself proclaimed Emperor in Italy and was raising a force to march on Byzantium. The new Emperor, Constantine IX, had put him in command of an army to counter Maniakes and had refused to let Harald return to Russia. Harald wanted a chance to enjoy his ill-gotten gains, so secretly purchased a number of galleys. One night he stole down with his personal followers boarded the galleys and sailed out into the Bosporus, then north through the Black Sea to the Dnieper and then on to Kiev.

Their sailing was covered by an attack on Byzantium by the forces of Yaroslav, who used intelligence that Harald had been supplying over the years. The overwhelming numbers of Russians should have carried the day. Byzantium, however, had a secret weapon—Greek Fire—which burnt even on water. Yaroslav's fleet went up in flames, fanned by a strong wind. It is said that there were over ten thousand Russian corpses washed up on shore. The defeat was complete when the Slav army commander, Vyshata, was ambushed during the retreat and the remnants of the army cut to pieces.

One of the charges brought against Harald was that he was giving information to Yaroslav to enable him to attack Constantinople, and there is no reason to doubt this. Harald's escape and Yaroslav's attack are just too fortuitous to be coincidence.

It looks more like a long-term plan to take over Constantinople by Yaroslav, Rurik's descendent. Scholars do not agree as to whether this was an old-fashioned Viking raid for booty or an attempt to take over the Eastern Roman Empire. My own opinion is the latter. Had it succeeded, then the Ulvungar dynasty would have achieved their aim of taking over the Eastern Empire before turning their attention to the Western Empire. With the wealth of Byzantium behind them, they would probably have been unstoppable.

Harald, meanwhile, returned to Kiev in triumph and asked for Yaroslav's daughter Elizabeth to be his wife. After some demure by the lady in question they were married late in 1043. Harald was twenty-eight and the most famous warrior of the moment. He had married into the Ulvungar dynasty and was related by marriage to King Henry I of France, husband to his wife's sister, Anna and with King Andrew of Hungary, husband of the other sister, Anastasia. Now it was time to return home to Norway with his new wife and his booty.

Chapter 9 References

1. Sawyer, B. & P. (1993) – *Medieval Scandinavia, from Conversion to Reformation, c. 800-1500*, p. 33-35.

2. Ibid., see also McLynn, F. *op. cit.* p. 41.

3. See Genealogy III in Chapter 7, the descent from Gorm, being his son Harold Bluetooth and grandson Sven Forkbeard.

4. Jerlow, L. G. (ed.) (1968) – *Ordo Niderosiensis Ecclesiae*, p. 124-128, Oslo.

5. McLynn, *op. cit.* p. 44.

6. Montgomery, H. (2003) – *The Normans in the South*, Lectures to U3A.

Chapter 10

The Goddess Line and the Sacred Triangle

In Chapter 2, I pointed out that Document 2 appeared to show a female as opposed to a male line of descent. I wondered if there was some sort of "Hidden Power" line via a female descent. This was further strengthened by the information set out in Chapter 8. If there was such a line, then it was going to be well nigh impossible to prove. But if I could show that it probably existed, it might in itself be proof of intention. In a world dominated by male genealogies there would be no better way of hiding this "Hidden Power" than by having it descend via the female line.

I decided, therefore, to make a start with Documents 1 and 2. Document 1 clearly states that Jesus' wife was Miriam of Bethany of the House of Saul. If Yuri and I were right, that Bethany represented Bithynia and that a group of Benjamites had finished up in Bithynia, then it was just possible that Mary did indeed descend from the daughter of Saul. Was there any evidence for this? Well, yes there was. In Samuel Book 2 it says that Michal, the daughter of Saul, who had been the wife of David, had married a second time to Phaltiel, the son of Laish. He had tried to follow her to David's House after David demanded her return, but he had been sent back.[1] It would be reasonable to infer that this couple had children and that therefore, a line of Saul survived, which would be very important to the Benjamites. (We must always bear in mind that they regarded themselves as the rightful Kings of Israel, even though they were probably kings of separate city-states.)

It is also probable that this group of Benjamites were not worshippers of a male deity but a female one. It was also likely that the person of Saul's daughter and her daughters in their turn, would be regarded as embodiments of the female deity, just as later, Cleopatra would be considered the embodiment of Isis. Now if this was so, then it was likely that there would be a continuation of females who would have to receive this "Hidden Knowledge" or Gnosis from another family member, in most cases her mother.

But there was one more document to look at. This was a document that had been known about for a long time and has been mentioned by other authors in various books.[2]

Document 4

"Now it came to pass in those days that a Priestess of the Goddess from the village of Bethany of the Tribe of Benjamin and a keeper of the Sacred Doves was affianced to a man called Jeshua for she had served her six years. Now Jeshua was of the House of David the King and they were married.

And Jeshua rebelled against the oppressors against Rome and was defeated, but many Romans were devotees of the Mother and were unwilling to kill her priestess who was with child. So Miriam took ship and was secretly smuggled into Gaul where she was delivered and there she abode many years. Now she bore a daughter who was exceedingly fair and the king of that place looked upon her and demanded that she be his wife but she was promised to the Goddess. But the king would not have it so and took her and made her his wife and she bore him a son and a daughter.

But the Goddess was exceeding wrath for his rape of her daughter and cursed him saying "Thy seed shall be estranged from me and thine inheritance taken from thee. They seed shall end by the piercing of an eye and so shall thine inheritance cease.

Yet for the sake of my priestess whom thou ravished shall I forgive thee and thy seed if they fulfill those labours which I shall give them.

They must fight and capture that which was lost to the oppressors of thy wife though they shall not hold it for they shall suffer betrayal (as thou betrayed me). Unless one of thy seed shall end the House of their betrayers by piercing the eye of its Liege. To this family shall I award greatness if they return to me and from this time to that shall be four and one hundred generations."

If one now puts this document together with Documents 1 and 2, a pattern emerges. A story that says that Mary of Bethany married Jesus and that "She" is of the House of Saul, a Benjamite. She was also, it seems, a priestess of the Goddess. A keeper of the sacred doves was a priestess of Isis, who was called Asherah in Israel. Originally, Asherah had been the wife or consort of Jahweh, before being edited out, but here we have a priestess who had served her six years and was now released, ready for marriage.

What is more, it confirms Document 2. Miriam does have a daughter, in Gaul, it now seems. That daughter marries a king, most probably a high-ranking officer in the service of Rome, with the Romanised name of Sigismundus. It is possible that this person was even a Jew in the service of Rome. This Miriam or Salome in turn has a daughter and a son. Yet the son has no known name. What is more, the line of Elchasai descends not from the unknown son but through the daughter, Ruth. In addition, only some three or four generations later the two Marthas are being "worshipped as Goddesses". Was it possible, therefore, that the Elchasai was only important as the consort of the female line?

If we went back to my hypothesis that John was "Elchasai" and that he had passed it on to Jesus, then John would have been Elchasai because of his wife. We know his wife's name, Anya, from the Mandeans and if you read the love poems he wrote to her, there is the distinct implication of worship on John's part. Admittedly, this could be simply poetic licence, but then again, perhaps not. But was Anya of the Benjamite line? It seemed as if it was the Benjamite females who were priestesses of the Goddess. It has been suggested that they were devotees of Isis, but I see no reason for this. Asherah had always been the consort of Jahweh. There exists a coin from the 1st century BC, which is clearly inscribed "Jahweh and his Asherah", much to the dismay of many Jewish Rabbis who would like to pretend that the Jews only worshiped "The Lord".

We had, however, no documentary evidence that John's wife had been a devotee of the Goddess. We did, however, have documentary evidence that Jesus' wife Miriam had been such a person, indeed she herself had been a priestess, a keeper of the sacred doves, who had served six years. I have assumed that the "six years" was an agreed period for a priestess to serve, but so far as I am aware, there is no other reference to six years in any other literature.

In view of the fact that the descendents of Miriam, the two Marthas, were being revered as Goddesses some centuries later, I think it not unreasonable to suppose that her other descendents, Miriam or Salome and Ruth are at least priestesses or embodiments of the Goddess Asherah, in their turn. I think it also reasonable to suggest that these Priestesses would ally themselves with Royal or Noble Houses in order to protect themselves and to proselytise their particular form of the Judaic/Christian Religion. It must also be emphasied that Jesus himself talked about the Mother Earth in both the Gospel of Peace of Jesus Christ and the later, fuller Gospel of the Essenes.[3]

One would be looking, therefore, for marriages to leaders who were either on top or who were likely to be on top. One would also expect to find these leaders supporting a female Godhead, either directly or indirectly. THE HUNT WAS ON.

The first obvious person after the two Marthas was their daughter or more likely great-granddaughter Maria. She certainly married into a kingly, not to say Godly, line. Indeed, if Ataulf was considered to be the embodiment of Odin, and Maria the embodiment of Asherah or perhaps the female consort of Odin, Freya, then this would make perfect sense.

There was, however, another pattern emerging, one that I have called the Sacred Love Triangle. The reason for its emergence was my discovering the real meaning of Jesus' last words on the cross. The words you may remember were "Eloi", or "Eli, Eli Lama Sabachthani". Hebrew and many of the Eastern Languages descend from an oral form of Sanskrit, so I decided to consult a Sanskrit Scholar.[4] Imagine my surprise to learn that this was indeed a form of Sanskrit called Prakrit, or the tongue of the Buddha. The actual words would be written today, Ila (pronounced Ela or Eli) Lama Sabachthani. Ila is a female name meaning Earth or "Mother Earth", Lama means "The Silent Ones" and Sabachthani means "We (specifically 3) speak with one voice". The words taken together would be, "Mother Earth, Earth Mother we the three silent ones speak with one voice". Now a Christian might say that the three are Father, Son and Holy Ghost— except for the reference to "Mother Earth", which rather stymies that particular idea. It would, however, have been perfectly in line with Essene doctrine and indeed, what Jesus himself taught.[5] To me it seemed obvious that Jesus was addressing the two Marys who were watching—Mary Magdelene and the other Mary (of Bethany), his two Consorts, or Earth Mothers. He is saying that the three speak with one voice and is bidding all to listen to them when he dies. So much for the Church being given into the hands of Peter!

The really amazing thing was that the pattern was to be repeated again and again in their descendents. Ataulf had married both Maria and Galla Placidia. Charlemagne had at least a wife and concubine, if not several at the same time. In the Odonic Line it was the norm, but it went on even after the so-called Christianisation of the Viking Dynasties and was connived at by the Church. Harald Hardrada had two wives at one and the same time. King Cnut was already married to Aelgifa of Northampton when he married Emma of Normandy in a Christian Church officiated, by a Bishop. Hrolf the Ganger was married to Gizelle but his children were by Poppa. William Longsword was married to Leutgarda but his heir was by Espriota. Richard I of Normandy was married to Emma and was also married by "Danish Rite" to Gunnora, Richard II was married to Judith of Brittany but also had children by Papia, Robert was handfasted to Estrith but his heir was by Herleve and so it went on—generation after generation. This was more than just a coincidence or the king taking advantage of the situation. This appeared to be a deliberate policy, indeed accepted by the women concerned, perhaps even encouraged by them. Certainly Emma of Normandy went willingly to Cnut's bed and may even have been the prime mover in the marriage, knowing that Cnut's first wife was still alive. Indeed, in this case there is a feeling that in order to legitimise his right to the throne of England Cnut had to marry her, the previous Queen of Ethelred, the "Earth Mother" and embodiment of the land.

If this was indeed a deliberate policy, then where did it originate? Was it an invention of John's or of Jesus'? I thought this unlikely and then remembered the article I had quoted earlier on the Sumerian deities in Chapter 1. Were, in fact, Ishtar and Innana simply different names for the Consort of Anu, or were they two separate female deities? Did Jaweh have one consort—Asherah, or was there more than one? I have already remarked that the word Elohim is feminine plural. It is interesting to note that the Shekhina, or angels covering the Ark of the Covenant, are actually a Talmudic term to denote God's manifestation on Earth in tangible form, although in Midrash literature the Shekhina were separate female entities embodying Wisdom. In other words, the Shekhina were a form of Earth Mothers.

According to the American academic, Raphael Patai, one of the functions of the Shekhina was to argue with God "in defense of Man", because of "her compassionate nature". In the Gnostic Gospels, Mary Magdelene carries out the same function.[6] Interestingly, some years ago when I was researching this book I was able to consult a copy of the Polyglot Bible kept by the Royal Grammar School, Guilford. What this Bible does is to use Latin as the language into which all other language Bibles are translated so that one can compare each language Bible to each other. St. John's Gospel was extremely interesting. In English its starts: "In the beginning was the Word", etc.; in Latin, "In Principio erat Verbum". In Provencal it says: "Lo filh era al comensament"; in Latin, "In Principio erat Filius" = "In the beginning was the Son." In Greek and Aramaic the word used is "Logos", meaning Wisdom or Understanding.[7] The implication here is "Sophia". So in this case, St. John's gospel, which was almost certainly originally written in Greek or Aramaic, would read in English, "In the beginning was Wisdom and Wisdom was with God and Wisdom was God"—and Wisdom is always considered to be feminine.

Patai also makes the point that the word Cherubim, in Hebrew, *K'rubh,* is thought to derive from the Akkadian/Sumerian word "karibu", meaning an intermediary between God and mankind, though Patai points out that "female genii" would be nearer the mark.

Glueck also points out that the Cherubim were frequently shown locked in unashamedly sexual embrace, which frequently caused the worshippers to join together in feverish consummation of fertility rites. This was particularly true of the Nabateans.[8] If again, as I have surmised earlier, Mary Magdelene was a Nabataean, then the jigsaw was starting to fall into place.

In was beginning to assume a definite picture. There was a triangle of one male and two females and it looked as if Jesus was saying that he was the embodiment of God. This was exactly what the earliest Christians maintained—that Jesus was the embodiment of God, but not God himself (The Arian Doctrine). He represented God on Earth and like God had two consorts—The Two Marys. This formed a pyramidal structure:

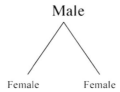

There should, however, be a balance because ancient religions usually had a balance. In other words, there should be another opposite structure:

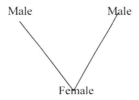

If it came from ancient Judaism, I would find it there. Sure enough, there it is for all to see:

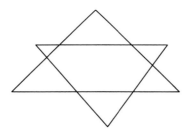

The Star of David or the Seal of Solomon.

The two triangles interlinked. David, we know, had married Michal, the daughter of Saul, but he had also married Ahinoam and Abigail, Nabal's wife the Carmelite. We also know that Michal had married again to Phaltiel and it would appear that Abigail was also Nabal's wife. So we had the dual triangle. One male and two females, and of those two females, two were also married to other men.[9] What is more,

Solomon was the son of David by Bath-Sheba (which means the daughter of Sheba), the wife of Uriah the Hittite, and was conceived whilst she was still married to Uriah. The interpolation that the first child died and that she then bore Solomon is a later "P" interpolation.[10]

Solomon too, had several wives as well as having an affair with the Queen of Sheba, (Sa'ba , Sabateans later Nabataeans), with whom he is supposed to have had a son, Menelik. What is more, both David and Solomon were always being accused by the male-orientated Jahwah-ites of worshiping other Gods, and particularly Asherah. We even have the case of incest between Amnon and Tamar.[11]

It seems likely, therefore, that Jesus was deliberately following in the ancient ways of his forefathers by having two wives, as did Herod. I also came to the conclusion that both women had anointed him but wondered if, in fact, the anointing of the "head" was a euphimism for anointing the phallus, as shown in the engraving on the temple at Luxor and as was to be seen on the great Temple at Philae, the Temple of the Benjamites.[12] It has been quite clear to scholars for some time that the original Judaic religion contained a considerable amount of sexual participation, both within and without the temple itself. The Gospel of the Carpocrations, according to Iranaeus, Bishop of Lyons also apparently contained secret sexual practices.

There was no information that I could find showing that either of the two Marys had other lovers or husbands, though there is a sugges-tion that Mary of Bethany later married a certain John, who may or may not have been John the Evangelist. There is some circumstantial evidence that Mary, the mother of Jesus, was married before to an elder brother of Joseph and that Mary-Jacob, Jesus' sister, may have been an elder half-sister.[13]   There is no document that shows the descendents of Mary Magdelene past that of a son and possible daugh-ter, though both Yuri and I are pretty sure it once existed, and possibly a copy will turn up some time. Certainly the Royal French House of Valois claim to be descended from her—though this may be an error on their part if they believed that Mary of Bethany and Mary Magdelene were one and the same. The truth is, they descend from the marriage of Yaroslav's daughter to King Henry I and, as I have shown, Yaroslav descends from the marriage of Ataulf and Maria.

It was also obvious why the descendents of Jesus and Mary of Bethany should ally themselves with the other great God dynasty of the Odonic line and interesting that both owed their ideas on religion at least in part from that of ancient Babylon. The Judaic side had taken at least part of their religion from the time they were captives in Babylon and the Odonic from their time as rulers in Babylon.

But there was yet another Triangulation in Judaic esoterica. It is called Kabbalah.

Its diagrammatic form is as follows:

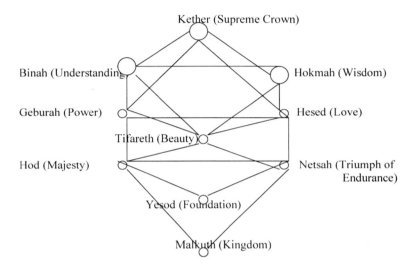

Etz Hay-Yim (Tree of Life)

I may get into trouble with Kabbalistic scholars for my next comment, but bear with me. If we take Kether as being the male Godhead and Binah and Hokmah as being the female forms of Wisdom and Understanding, then we have the top triangle. Admittedly, Hokmah is generally seen as a bearded man but this has not always been the case, and Binah has always been a mature woman, whilst Kether is always a male king.

At the bottom of the Tree is Malkuth, representing Mother Earth, who is usually seen as a young woman crowned and seated on a throne. One would expect, therefore, that Hod and Netsah would be male but in fact, they are somewhat different. Hod is usually seen as an Hermaphrodite, whilst Netsah is normally a beautiful nude woman. This is because Yesod, which forms the other triangle with Hod and

Netsah, is usually a handsome nude man. In turn Tifareth is clearly
female, though often shown as an infant (Motherhood) or as a sacrificial God (gender non-specific). I have always regarded Tifareth as
female and as her aspect is beauty, she is the base of the triangle with
Geburah and Hesed, which are usually shown as a warrior driving a
chariot and a king on a throne, respectively.

One of the great exponents of Kabbalah during the middle ages was
Rabbi Moses, the Elder Kalonymides of the House of the Makhirs of
Septimania, who himself became Nasi. In fact, for much of the Middle
Ages, Kabbalistic Judaism was the mainstream of Jewish thought. The
idea of the sacred triangle was therefore something that would have
been regarded as normal. The first Nasi himself had had two wives and
we know that Charlemagne had at least two at the same time. It
seemed to me that it was therefore something that went with being a
Jewish Prince or Princess, as well as being the norm in the Odonic line.
No wonder these two lines found so much in common. We knew that
their descendents, the Ulvungar Dynasty, in the male line generally
had either two wives or a wife and concubine, but the women had also
confirmed the lower triangle (two male and one female).

With the Church in the ascendent at this period any affairs by ladies
of high rank were going to have to be kept secret from the prying eyes
of priests and the general public. For a woman of rank to have a husband and lover was to court disaster. If I was to find any, it would have
to be in the areas of the old Visigothic Kingdoms and Septimania. Sure
enough, the literature showing this was there. It was called the
Chansons of the Troubadours and was presided over by two great
ladies, Ermengarde of Narbonne (the centre of Septimania), and
Eleanor of Aquitaine (died 1204), whose lands included much of the
old Visigothic Kingdom of Toulouse. Married to Henry II of England,
she bore him a number of children, including the famous Richard,
Coeur de Lion. Henry himself had a mistress, in fact, the girl who
should have been his eldest son's wife, but it appears that Eleanor also
had a lover, one Bernart de Ventadour (though some authorities doubt
this). I came to the conclusion that it was likely that Bernard was her
lover, that her husband was aware of this and that it was probably the
inability of some of my distinguished colleagues to accept the idea that
a Queen might have a lover. That was the problem, even though they
accepted quite happily that Henry had a mistress.

Indeed, the whole concept of the Troubadour love poems was the worshipping of an embodiment of womanhood, normally the wife of one's Lord. Indeed, it seems that the *Chansons of the Troubadours* were not just celebrating the feminine Godhead, which many other authors have mentioned, but were deliberately celebrating the female half of the sacred love triangle. Guillaume IX of Aquitaine (1071-1127) was the first of these troubadours whose work has survived. Some of Guillaume's poems are so bawdy that they have never been translated into English and today would be considered pornographic if written in English. They celebrate sexual love in all its fantasies. But Guillaume goes further, a Lady (i.e. The wife of the Lord) "commits a great and mortal sin if she does not love a loyal knight". Furthermore, he appeals for the release of physical consummation. Later a new class of troubadour emerges—that of Bernart de Ventadour, mentioned above, and Count Eblo II. In these poems the troubadour pines for physical love, but theoretically at least, never attains it. Again, I think this was either the fear of the Church or the fear of their Lord if he did not like it.[14]

All of those areas which had seen the influence of the Odonic, Elchasaic and Visigothic families showed this flowering of the Troubadours; Poitiers, Provence, Ventadour, Narbonne, Limoges and Orange all became, in their turn, centres of the worship of the feminine triangle.

There was another thing that surfaced at this time, which again has been totally misunderstood by the puritanic and made much of by Holywood. The so-called "Droit de Seigneur" was not that a Lord had the right to take any woman on her wedding day, but that any of his female tenants could ask to come to his bed on their wedding night and for one night become the Goddess incarnate, physically worshipped by their Lord and Master. The Church tried to stop this practice, which they regarded as a remnant of paganism, but it persisted in some places.

Eventually this flowering was cut down and wiped out by the Church's campaign against the Cathars, the inheritors of the Elchasites, known as the Albigensian Crusade.

There is, however, another aspect to the document I had quoted earlier (Document 3) and that is the business of the piercing of the eye and a sacrificial king. In Norse mythology, Odin gains supreme power, knowledge and wisdom by giving up an eye at the Well of Mimir. He also gained control of the runes of power by being nailed to the great Tree, Yggdrasil, for nine nights and nine days. Odin's Rune Song goes as follows:

> I know that I hung
> On a wind-rocked tree
> Nine whole nights,
> With a spear wounded
> And to Odin offered
> Myself to myself;
> On that tree
> Of which no one knows
> From what root it springs.

Once again, the comparison with Jesus is uncanny. Jesus hangs on a cross and has a spear thrust into his side. Odin hangs on the Tree Yggdrasil and is wounded with a spear. Odin comes down and becomes King of the Gods and Allfather. Jesus comes down and is supposedly resurrected as God, becoming one with God the Father. Small wonder that Jesus' descendents linked up with the Odonic line, with which they had so much in common.

There is yet another curious affinity. The Symbol of Odin is called the Valknot or Knot of the Slain:

Once again the triangles appear, this time three times three.

Jesus' son-in-law[15] is threatened by the Goddess that he will die by having his eye pierced or, if not him, then his descendents will die out as a result, unless they perform certain tasks. At the time that Maria married Ataulf, he was fighting the Romans, just what the Goddess had commanded Mary's descendents to do. So by marrying Ataulf, Maria was conforming to the Family requirement. What is more they captured and sacked Rome itself, taking with them to their Visigothic kingdom some of the treasures looted by the Romans from the Temple in Jerusalem. In fact, we know from Roman records that they took the seven-branched candalabra (Menorah). This must have seemed the answer to the Elchasaic dilemma, but there was also another Rome, the Rome of the East, called Constantinople. So just to be on the safe side, when opportunity offered, another descendent of the Ulvungars, Elizabeth, was married to Harald Hardrada, the person who gouged out the eyes of the Eastern Roman Emperor, Michael, thus ending the House of their betrayers! In fact, Harald himself was a considerable poet and wrote some of his best verses in praise of Elizabeth, including one that refers to her as "The Goddess of the Golden Ring".[16] I know there are those who will say this was normal poetic licence and under any other circumstances I would agree, but when all the bits of a jigsaw puzzle fit together, then and only then will the true picture emerge. Jesus, like Odin, had hung on a tree or cross and like Odin had thereby gained wisdom.

Elizabeth allowed Harald to take a second wife, on their return to Norway and upon Harald's death in the Battle of Stamford Bridge in 1066, she took a lover herself—again, the dual triangle.

I am aware that there are those who will attribute the eye piercing to Dagobert, the so-called last of the Merovingians, however, as I have shown earlier, the Merovingians were not direct Elchasaic descendents, though they were Odonic. Nor, so far as I am aware, is there any proof that Dagobert was so killed.

There are, however, two other interesting events that are historically vouched for. The first is the "accidental" killing of King Henry II of France by Gabrial de Montgomery. Gabriel was certainly both an Elchasaic and an Odonic descendent and Henry was certainly his liege. There were also rumours at the time that Gabriel was the Queen's lover and that at least one of her children was by him. This would, of course, make the Sacred Triangle complete.

The other event was the killing of Harold Godwinsson, King of England, with an arrow to the eye. There is some doubt as to whether he was killed in this way, but it is possible that the Norman Families, who would have known about this curse, would have made out that Harold was killed in this way in order to try to overcome the curse.

But the Church was becoming more and more powerful and oppressive, so the Goddess worship had to be hidden. In Norman England, apart from the help given to Jews, there was also a flowering of "Lady" chapels. That is Churches and Chapels dedicated to "Our Lady of XXX", without specifying who the Lady was. The Church could assume it was Mary, the Mother of Jesus, whilst its builders might know it as Mary, the Wife of Jesus or even Mary, the wife of Ataulf, descendent of Elchasai.

Of one thing we can be sure of—a line of female knowledge continued well into the High Middle Ages and into the time of Rene d'Anjou and the Medicis.

Chapter 10 References.

1. The Second Book of Samuel, Chap. 3 v. 14-16.

2. Baigent, M. Leigh, R. Lincoln, H. (1996) – *The Holy Blood and the Holy Grail*, p. 487-488, Arrow Books, London. See also *The Temple and the Lodge*, by the same authors. See also Montgomery, H., *Montgomery Millennium op. cit.* p. 49. Also Reilly, G. *op. cit.* documents published in 1820.

3. Szekely, E. & Weaver, P. (1986) – The Gospel of Peace of Jesus Christ, C. Daniel Co., Ltd., Saffron Walden, Essex, UK.

4. Sri Anando Mukerjee Dev Sarma.

5. The Gospel of the Essenes, p. 52, including the Gospel of Peace of Jesus Christ, but other references as well; see also Appendix 3.

6. Patai, R. (1990) – *The Hebrew Goddess*, p. 25, Detroit.

7. The Bishop of Oxford, Rt. Rev. Richard Harries, says that the word "Logos" could equally mean wisdom. "In the beginning was wisdom, and wisdom was with God and wisdom was God." Harries, R. (1993) – *Art and Beauty of God*, pp. 67, 72-7, Mowbray, London & New York.

8. Glueck, N. (1965) – *Deities and Dolphins, The Story of the Nabataeans*, p. 166, New York.

9. Samuel II, Chap. 2 v. 2 & Chap. 3 v. 15.

10. Samuel II, Chaps. 11 & 12.

11. Samuel II, Chap. 13.

12. Macquitty, W. (1976) – *The Island of Isis*, photo opp. p. 76, also Chap. 4, "Philae", Book Club Associates, London. The hieroglyphs on Philae were painstakingly drawn by my late brother-in-law, J. A. Chubb, before the waters covered the site.

13. In the Gospel of Philip, p. 65 it says Mary his mother, the sister of his mother, and Miriam of Magdala. It then goes on to call his mother's sister the sister of Jesus. It occurred to me that in many languages "of" and "by" are the same word and that an alternate translation might be, "The sister by his mother", implying Mary had been married before. This is reinforced by his sister's name, Mary-Jacob, indicating that her father was Jacob and she was his only child. In which case, her marriage to Joseph would have been a Leverite Marriage.

14. For the whole discussion on the Troubadours see Barber, R. (1970) – *The Knight and Chivalry*, Longman, London.

15. Apparently refers to Sigismundus, son-in-law to Jesus from Odonic myth.

16. The *Gamanvisur*, series of Skaldic Verses, by Harald Hadrada.

Chapter 11

The Pesher Code

The problem with Documents 1, 2, 3, & 4 is that although they may well be translated from earlier documents, none of them in the form I have used them pre-date 1750. If, therefore, they are to have any validity to the historian it must be shown that either these existed in some form at or about the time of the events they record, or that at least they were known about at that time. So the provenance given in Appendix 2 is very important.

In 1947 two Arab boys discovered the first of what would come to be known as the Dead Sea Scrolls. Later discoveries were made in 1952 and 1954. I do not wish here to go into the appalling arrogance of the Church and the way they refused to let scholars have access to the scrolls. Several books have been written about it including Eisenman and Wise's introduction to *The Dead Sea Scrolls Uncovered*.[1] In this book they make clear that the early Judaic-Christians, sometimes called the Ebionites and descended from the original Jerusalem Church of James the Just, brother of Jesus, did not consider Jesus to be divine. On the contrary, they made clear that Joseph was his real blood father and that he and Mary had had Jesus quite normally. It is further made clear in other documents that Jesus married and had children.[2] Furthermore, they show that the Essenes, far from being a group of devout pacifists were, in fact, a group of religious zealots preparing to wage Holy War on Rome. Indeed, modern Islamic terror tactics and the concept of Matyrdom for God's Justice can be clearly seen in some of the Scrolls.[3]

In 1992 Dr. Barbara Thiering published a book called *Jesus the Man*. Barbara Thiering and Tom Morrison had worked together on the Dead Sea Scolls and Thiering's book goes even further than that of Eisenman & Wise. In it she proves beyond reasonable doubt that Jesus was a member of the Essenes, that John the Baptist was at one stage the Zadok priest of the Essenes, and that both John and Jesus were married, the latter twice. The method of working this out is called the *Pesher Code* and it depends upon the fact that the Essenes were obliged to hide much of their "Wisdom" under a code for fear of the Romans, and indeed to keep their secrets from prying eyes. Those in the know knew the real facts, whilst those who did not understand were taught in terms of parables and mysteries. "Those who have eyes to see let them see." Thus, the Romans are referred to as Babylon or Kittim. Caesar means Herod unless it is preceeded by a name such as Tiberius, when it then refers to the Roman Emperor. I do not intend to go into details of her work, as one can read it for oneself.[4] My only disagreement with her (and then only because of the previous documents) is that she thinks that Mary of Bethany and Mary Magdelene are one and the same person and that Jesus' second wife was called Lydia, whilst I believe that Lydia and Mary Magdelene are one and the same and that Mary of Bethany is separate. In my opinion, had Dr. Thiering been aware of the other documents, she would have been in agreement with me. To a large extent, however, the names of Jesus' wives are unimportant. What is important is that there exists another body of documents, in this case the Dead Sea Scrolls and the "Pesher" reading of the New Testament, that bears these documents out.

In her book she maintains that each marriage had two parts. What she calls "The First Marriage" and what I term the "Handfasting" (or engagement period, which was formalised by a Kettubah) was first. Some time later, in the case of Essenes—she maintains it was three years later—we have the second part of the marriage, which she calls "The Second Marriage". At this time, sexual consummation took place. In her book Dr. Thiering also makes the point that Jesus' own birth is called into question because he was conceived during the "Engagement" period and that at least some of the Essenes preferred his brother James as the rightful Davidic heir. We saw this earlier with the Septimania Makirs. For Jesus to overcome this problem he must make the right marriage. Thiering suggests that the story in Mark 5 regarding the daughter of Jairus is the initiation ceremony of Mary Magdelene, however I think that this is, in fact, her handfasting. Dr. Thiering says Mary married late because this ceremony was her rebirth at age twelve or thirteen, but I think that Mary was to marry fully at age 15 or 16. This would have been the norm for that period, and I believe that this ceremony was the Kettubah or handfasting, with the final marriage to take place 3 months later.

In Mark's Gospel, Chap. 5, Jesus enters the house of Jairus with three witnesses and the father and mother of the girl in question. He raises her with the words "Talitha Cumi", which the Gospel says means, "Damsel, I say unto thee arise." But "Talitha Cumi" actually means, "My Soul is Yours" (or "your Soul is mine")[5], hence Dr. Thiering's belief that this was a ceremony of rebirth according to the rituals of the Essenes. However, Dr. Thiering is a Christian and perhaps not aware of the form of the Kettubah, which was in use by 100 BC[6] and was written by Rabbi Hillel, one of the founders of the Essenes.[7] The groom would enter the house of the bride with two witnesses and, in front of the High Priest, the groom and the father of the bride would sign the Kettubah. The bride would then enter veiled and sit on a chair or stool. The groom would hand her the Kettubah and possibly some money, and then raise her veil with the words, "Arise, your Soul (or you) are consecrated to me".

We can go further than this, however, because the Jairus Priest at the time was John the Baptist[8] and we know that Mary of Bethany was not his daughter. Barbara Thiering quite rightly identifies her as Mary Magdelene, confirming my point that Mary Magdelene was John the Baptist's daughter. I would suggest, therefore, that this indicates that Mary Magdelene and Mary of Bethany are not the same person and that this is, in fact, Mary Magdelene's handfasting ceremony. Furthermore, just after this event John is thrown into prison and sends the message to Jesus, as I have outlined in Chapter 3. When John is beheaded, his followers, plus Jesus and Mary Magdelene, have to flee to the desert to take refuge, possibly in the caves at Qumran, as Barbara Thiering suggests. Mary would be 13 or 14—certainly mature enough by the standards of the time to have consummated the marriage, and this may well have happened, with a son being born perhaps a year later in Thyatira, where she went to give birth.[9]

I would suggest that what then happens is that Jesus needs to marry Mary of Bethany for both dynastic and political reasons and that this second full marriage, three years after their initial engagement, takes place in 33 AD. Thiering has identified this as taking place on 18th March, 33 AD at Ain Feshkha, at the house of Simon the Leper—otherwise Lazarus, brother of Mary of Bethany. The Nard perfume with which Mary anoints Jesus is a reference to a liturgy from the Song of Solomon, the Davidic House's marriage rite. "The House was filled with the fragrance of Nard."[10] It is noticeable that Judas offered an objection to this marriage, though the reason is not given. I suggest that his reason is Jesus' previous "marriage" to Lydia or Mary Magdelene.[11]

The *Pieta*, ca 1470-1475 by Giovanni Bellini. Jesus being resuscitated by his father, Joseph of Arimathea, Nicodemus and Mary of Bethany. Did he survive the crucifixion?

It is worthwhile reiterating here that until Pope Gregory I decreed that Mary of Bethany and "The Magdelene" were one and the same person, they had always been considered separate and even to this day the Eastern Orthodox consider them separate. (See Appendix 3.) It is possible, therefore, that originally the Magdelene had not been called Mary but Lydia, and that it is only since Gregory's intervention that she became known as Mary Magdelene.

Importantly, Thiering shows that Jesus did not die on the cross but was saved and continued his work of trying to bring the Jewish religion back to what he believed it should be, and against the strict doctrine of some of the Essenes. Hence, the Dead Sea Scrolls refer to him as "The Man of Lies"[12] whilst John the Baptist is referred to as "The Teacher of Righteousness."[13] However, after the debacle of the Jewish uprising, Jesus leaves Jerusalem with Mary of Bethany and later returns to Lydia or Mary Magdelene with whom he has another child in March, AD 51.

Dan Brown's *The Da Vinci Code* is a fictional novel about the bloodline of Jesus but in reality, fact is stranger than fiction.

If we put all the information that we have from various sources, The Dead Sea Scrolls, The Nag Hammadi Documents, The Berlin Manuscript and others mentioned in the text, we can come up with a reasonably accurate genealogical tree as follows:

The Family of Jesus from All Sources – 1
House of Saul (Benjamite)

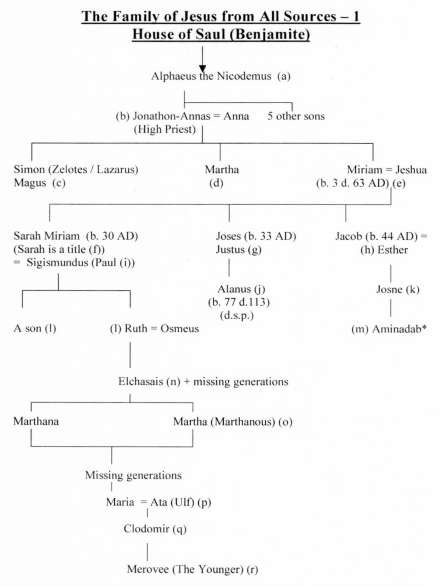

*Aminadab = Amun + Adab (or memory) = Amun is remembered. A name from St. Luke as being part of the Genealogy of Jesus and pre-David period.

The parenthetical letters indicate the relevant notes in Appendix 4 for this page and the next.

Family of Jesus from All Sources – 2

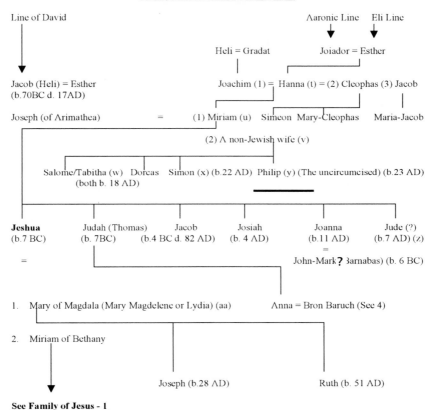

See Family of Jesus - 1

Nabatean Royal House

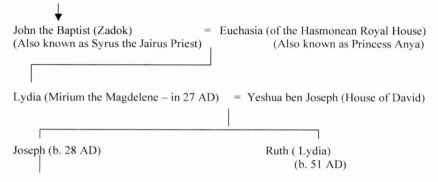

John the Baptist (Zadok)   = Euchasia (of the Hasmonean Royal House)
(Also known as Syrus the Jairus Priest)   (Also known as Princess Anya)

Lydia (Mirium the Magdelene – in 27 AD)   = Yeshua ben Joseph (House of David)

Joseph (b. 28 AD)   Ruth (Lydia)
                                            (b. 51 AD)

Josne (Believed born in Baghdad – Line of Exilarchs)

Family of Jesus 3

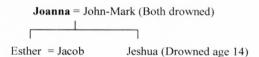

Joanna = John-Mark (Both drowned)

Esther = Jacob   Jeshua (Drowned age 14)

Family of Jesus 4

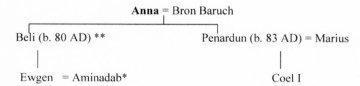

Anna = Bron Baruch

Beli (b. 80 AD) **   Penardun (b. 83 AD) = Marius

Ewgen   = Aminadab*   Coel I

**Beli is a Benjamite name, see Eisenman & Wise p. 47, proves Benjamite descent.

* Aminadab, Davidic line name.

Special Note: These genealogies are provisional and further research continues which may result in changes.

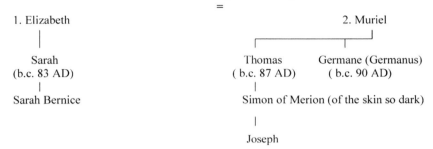

Family of Jesus 5
(Possible Elchasaic Line)

John Martinus (b. 53/54 AD)
=

1. Elizabeth   2. Muriel

Sarah   Thomas   Germane (Germanus)
(b.c. 83 AD)   (b.c. 87 AD)   (b.c. 90 AD)

Sarah Bernice   Simon of Merion (of the skin so dark)

                                                        Joseph

We can show, therefore, that the "Pesher" reading of the Dead Sea Scrolls and the New Testament are broadly in agreement with the documents I have outlined previously, though I have some differences of opinion with Barbara Thiering. In particular, I do not think that Jesus kept the celibate life of the Essenes once the more strict of their members had declared that his brother James was the rightful "David" and not Jesus. Nor do I think that the documents necessarily indicate a three-year period between birth of a child and resumption of sexual intercourse. The problem with ancient Hebrew is that there was only one past tense and one future tense and frequently the words for YEAR—MONTH—DAY were interchanged. Rabbi Hillel's (again, he was one of the founders of the Essenes) instructions to a Jewish husband are quite clear. "You must refrain from sexual intercourse with your wife for three months after she has given birth". I suggest, therefore, that the celibate period was three months, not three years. Having said that, the births themselves seem to show a three year period between births in many cases, but this does not allow for still births or deaths shortly after birth, which you would expect to see at this time.

There is, however, another document which indicates that this history and genealogy was known about during the Middle Ages and specifically during the period 1150-1220. This was the great song of the Medieval Troubadours known as the Grail Cycle. I do not intend to go into the Chrétien de Troyes cycle but will concentrate purely on those poems written by the most famous of the Medieval Troubadours, Wolfram von Eschenbach. These were *Parzival* and *Titurel*. Nor am I going to get into a discussion as to whether Wolfram or another poet called Albrecht wrote the last bit of the last of these poems, essentially from my point of view that is irrelevant. What is important is that the events at the time of Jesus were known about in detail at least until 1200, and that the persons writing these poems maintained that they had the information from documents that they had either seen, or were in their possession or that of their patrons.[14]

In order to show that Wolfram had access to real documents we must first prove that he had the opportunity to do so and that he showed that the documents were known to exist. We know, for example, that Wolfram went out to Outremer to visit the Templars and may well have been a secret Templar. (See note 17.) In *Titurel*, Wolfram gives a genealogy for Titurel. Titurel's great-grandfather is called Senabor and is supposed to be the Ruler of Cappadocia. His grandfather is Barillus. His great-grandfather may have been at Jesus' baptism and his grandfather and brothers were early Christians. His father was Titurisonne. His grandfather was a Roman and married the daughter of the Emperor Vespasian.[15] He was given the land of France by Vespasian and his brothers were given Anjou and Cornwall repectively.

This then would be his pedigree:

Titurel's Ancestry

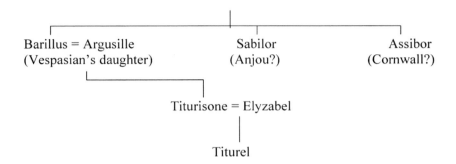

Senabor (Ruler of Cappadocia)

Barillus = Argusille   Sabilor   Assibor
(Vespasian's daughter)   (Anjou?)   (Cornwall?)

Titurisone = Elyzabel

Titurel

Is there any historical person whose history we know who measures up to this? Well, yes, there is! He was known as Josephus and he wrote *The Jewish Antiquities* and *The Jewish War*, from which we derive most of our knowledge for the period 100 BC to 100 AD. As I have mentioned before, he was born Joseph ben Mattathias in Palestine of a wealthy priestly house. His father Mattathias was the High Priest opposite the Esau of Cappadocia[16] and probably witnessed Jesus' baptism by John the Baptist at Qumrun. He was educated in Rome and returned to Galilee to become governor and commander of the Jewish troops against the Romans. He was defeated, captured and taken to the Emperor Vespasian. He became very friendly with the Imperial Family and was made a Roman citizen and adopted into the Imperial Family, taking the name Flavius Josephus, Flavius being the surname of the Imperial Family. He divorced his Jewish wife and married a Roman heiress, a distant relative of the Imperial Family. He had a son called Titus, named after the son of Vespasian.

This is Josephus's ancestry:

Josephus's Ancestry

Mattathias (High Priest)
(The priestly opposite of Esau of Cappadocia –
The Herodian Crown Prince)

|

Joseph
(Later Flavius Josephus)
= 1. Jewish wife (Divorced)
2. Roman heiress (Cousin of Vespasian)

|

Flavius Titus secundus

|

Son (Titurel? – Little Titus)

There is a further hint that Titurel is the grandson of Josephus. In the saga both Titurel and his father live for 500 years. Now as nobody believed that then, it is in fact indicating that you should take off 1000 years from the date, e.g. 1160 – 1000 = 160 AD. We know that Josephus died in 100 AD, so 160 AD would be precisely the time that Little Titus or Titurel would have been around.

There is, however, another character in both *Parzival* and *Titurel* who seems to be very important and indeed, whose exploits take up almost as much space as Parzival and Titurel even though the epics are not named after him. This person is Gahmuret. We know, from the same code as mentioned above, that these exploits also took place in the First century AD because Titurisone brought back the news of Gahmuret's death and it is obvious that Gahmuret was older than Titurisone. This person, Gahmuret, was a great warrior who fought for both Christians and Heathens. In the sagas the heathens are referred to as "Saracens", but again I think this was a code for "Jews".

Gahmuret marries twice—once and firstly to Belacane who is a "Black Queen" and secondly to Herzleide, who is a White Queen. By Belacane he has a son, Feirefiz, and by Herzleide another son, Parzival, after whom the first book is named. Feirefiz is said to be piebald or, in other words, half-caste. Parzival does not know his half-brother until they meet in battle. They are, however, after an enormous struggle, reconciled and they go off together to search for the grail.[17] This shows that Josephus's *Jewish War* and/or *Antiquities* were well known in the medieval period and it seems likely that the source for this may well have been the Knights Templar.

It would seem, therefore, in spite of the Albigensian Crusade, in which the Church tried to wipe out all knowledge of Jesus' marriage and the fact he had children, that at least the reality was known to some as late as 1200 AD. Okay, they had to cover it up in epic poetry of knightly deeds, but once again it was possible to find the truth if you knew the code.

In the battle, Feirefiz is said to have the Ecidemon or Angel of Man shining above his head, a clear reference to his being descended from Jesus. Once again we can show the two genealogies and compare them.

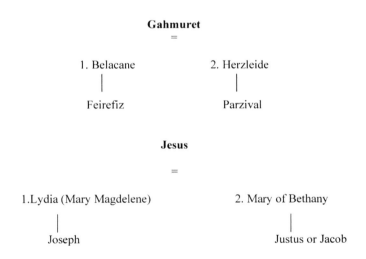

Gahmuret
=

1. Belacane   2. Herzleide

Feirefiz   Parzival

Jesus
=

1.Lydia (Mary Magdelene)   2. Mary of Bethany

Joseph   Justus or Jacob

To summerise, we have several different sources for the fact that Jesus was not only married, but married twice, and that those marriages had descendents whom we can identify today. These descendents married into the Odonic line. Both Odin and Jesus had hung on a tree and to an extent their "Wisdom" stemmed from this, and both had been pierced by a spear whilst on the tree. The New Testament is written in a code which is capable of being read by those who can understand it and this code is confirmed by the Dead Sea Scrolls. The Church has tried desperately to keep these facts a secret but these secrets were known to the Elchasaites and their spirituel descendents, the Cathars and Bogomils. After the Albigensian Crusade the secrets were thought to have been lost, but enough documents have survived to give us the real picture.

Chapter 11 References:

1. Eisenman, R. & Wise, M. (1992) – *The Dead Sea Scrolls Uncovered*, Penguin, London.
2. Ibid.
3. Ibid.
4. Thiering, B. (1992) – *Jesus The Man*, BCA, London.
5. Italics are mine.
6. Schneid, H. (1973) – *Marriage*, Keter Books, Jerusalem.
7. Mishnah Hag.2:2, Mt. 7:12 Also Thiering, p. 352.
8. Thiering, *op. cit.*, p. 420 note 9.
9. Ibid., p. 148. Mary Magdelene became the Head (Bishop) of the Thyatira Virgins, an order of Holy Whores or Harlots who practised sexual ecstacy as a form of religious worship. Hence her being called a Harlot. (Ibid., p. 59).
10. Ibid., p. 104.
11. Ibid., p. 104.
12. Ibid., p. 47 – quoting 1QpHab 2:2, 5:11, 10:9, 1QH 2:31, CD 1:15, 8:13, 19:26, 20:1 (these are the references to particular scrolls).
13. Ibid., p. 66.
14. Ibid., p. 41.
15. For full discussion see study by Charles Passage in *Titurel*, Frederick Ungar Publishing, New York.
16. Thiering, *op. cit.* p. 305.
17. Godwin, M. (1994) – *The Holy Grail*, p. 174-175, BCA Books, London.

Chapter 12

The Last Pieces of the Jigsaw

Generally speaking, most scholars accept that two or more pieces of evidence from different sources establish the probability of that event or person.

I started this book with pieces of a jigsaw. I have shown, I hope, that there is reasonable evidence to support the idea that the Goths were originally from Mesopotamia. There is documentary evidence that the Goths split and that part of that original tribe became known as the Visigoths. The history of the Visigoths is well documented in Latin and Greek and the names of their rulers are able to be confirmed in most cases. It is probable that there was not one Odin, but that this was a title held by the Chief or King of the Visigoths, used as the embodiment of Odin. We have also shown that there is an undisputable descent from Rhoes the Weoôulgeot to the House of Brocus.

I have also shown that the Old Testament is not the actual history of a people called the Israelites. That it is unlikely to have been written until the Babylonian Captivity and its aftermath, and that much of the early parts owe more to Babylonian Mythology than historical data.

We have together explored documents, some of which first saw the light of day again in the mid-17th century. Since then more and more documents have been discovered including that body of documents usually called the Dead Sea Scrolls. That in spite of the Church's attempts to destroy or hide them, there exist documents showing Jesus not as a heavenly Messiah, but as a good Jewish man, who married and had children, whose descendents are still with us.

Indeed, the Church historian Eusebius confirms the existence of descendents of Jesus and his family at least until 318 AD, when eight descendents visited Rome and spoke with "Pope" Sylvester. The Jesuit Professor, Malachai Martin, who was professor at Rome under Pope Paul XXIII and who had access to Vatican documents, has gone further and identified the eight members of the delegation, identifying seven by name and the eighth by implication. One of them was a direct descendent of Jesus who, in the words of Pope Sylvester, had the "facial characteristics that Jesus himself would have born".[1]

I and my collegue, Dr. Margaret Tottle-Smith, have shown that Jesus himself was one of the Elchasais and that he was party to a hidden tradition, which included the use of the language of the Buddha. That the families of the Odonic God-Kings and the God-Kings of Israel merged into the House of Brocus with the marriage of Maria to Ataulf, and we have been able to tentatively identify the missing generations within the Elchasaic line as follows:

Tentative Elchasaic Line from Jesus

Jeshua den Joseph = Miriam of Bethany

Daughter (Miriam?) = Sigismundus (Saul/Paul)

Ruth = Osmeus(2) (John Matinus)

Thomas

Simeon
(Of the skin, so dark)

Joseph

Jonathon

The two Marthas

Jacob
(Who was one of the delegates to Pope Syvester in 318 AD)

Joseph

John Cassian(3)
(Who preached to Alaric and Ataulf)

Maria = Ataulf

It is easy to see how the Odonic Line would have accepted and protected the Davidic Line of Jesus. Odin had hung on a tree, been pierced in the side with a spear, had survived and had become a very wise man or sage. Jesus had hung on a cross or tree, been pierced in the side, had survived and become a great sage or prophet. Jesus was apparently acceptable to most Europeans whilst as Odin was no longer. *So let us accept the New Odin—Jesus Christ—and let the two lines become merged into the New God Kings!*

I have shown the origins of the Ulvungar rulers of England and Normandy and for those interested it is possible to trace a line of descent, frequently via a female line, to the present British Royal Family.

King Stephen (1135-1154) inherited his claim via Adela, the daughter of William I.

Henry II (1154-1189) inherited via Matilda, who certainly conformed to the sacred triangle. The claim of Henry VII came through Margaret Beaufort. In Scotland the claims of both the Balliols and Bruces came via females, and that of the House of Steward (Stuart) came via Marjorie, the daughter of King Robert. Most famously, James I & VI inherited through his mother, Mary Queen of Scots, and she was an Ulvungar/Elchasaic descendent on both the male and female side.

As a matter of interest, the kings of England up until the time of Charles I were always served by the highest in the land on their knees, just as the God-Kings of Thailand are today. When Charles I talked of the "Divine Right" of kings, to what was he referring—the anointing by the Church or his own divine descent?

When the Oligarchs of Britain decided to replace the Stuarts, it still did not occur to them to go outside of the "Sacred Blood". So when the House of Orange came to the throne it was because of Mary and when, in turn, they were replaced with the House of Hanover, this was due to descent from Sophia. Of course some of the most famous of the countries' rulers have been females—Elizabeth of England, Victoria of Great Britain and our present Queen.

However, it is not just the Rulers of Britain who have the blood of the God-Kings in them—so too, do the Valois Family of France and the Scandinavian Dynasties. The Romanovs of Russia are descended from Rurik, as was Prince Paul of Yugoslavia.

It is interesting to note that at Queen Victoria's Diamond Jubilee, all of Europe, most of Africa and most of the Middle and Far East were ruled by descendents of the House of Brocus. Iraq, the place from which they had come as God-Kings, was under the British Crown and indeed was governed from British India. They had replaced the Romans and recaptured Jerusalem. They had achieved what they had set out to do just over 1000 years before! Fanciful? Let the facts speak for themselves.

And what of the "Sacred Triangle"? Queen Elizabeth I certainly had a lover who was also married. Mary Queen of Scots had both a husband and lover, and her husband Lord Darnley was known to have a mistress. The Hanoverians were notorious for having both wife and mistress and in the case of George IV, two wives. Edward VII had both wife and mistress. Edward VIII's mistress was still married to Mr. Simpson when she started her affair with Edward and only after the king's abdication did she marry Edward and become Duchess of Windsor. There were even rumours that she and Edward lived in a ménage a trois.

In more modern time one has to look no further than Prince Charles, Diana and Camilla and Camilla's husband, Brig. Parker-Bowles, to realise that the "Sacred Triangle" still rules the lives of the descendents of the Ulvungar/Elchasaic dynasties. Are they aware of it, or is it something ingrained in their genes? I do not know, I merely point out the facts.

And that, gentle reader, brings our jigsaw to completion. I hope that you have enjoyed reading it and piecing it together with me.

Chapter 12 References:

1. Martin, M., *op. cit.*, pp. 42-50.

2. Osmeus is an early form of local Latin similar to modern Portuguese and simply means "Theirs", indicating a member of the Desposyni. John Matinus was believed in the early Christian period to be the last son of Jesus by Mary Magdelene. In some versions he was born on Iona. I suspect that he was actually a first half-cousin of Ruth, but of the Magdelene line, hence his grandson being known as "Simeon of the skin so dark". The Aethiopian characteristics obviously come out from time to time. John Martinus's gr.-gr.- gr.-gr.-grandson Jacob attended as part of the delegation that went to see Pope Sylvester in AD 318. (See note 1.)

3. John Cassian, before becoming a desert father, raped a Jewish Lady of High Birth who became pregnant and had a daughter called Maria. She died at birth and in remorse John, with his father and young daughter, took refuge with a group of desert fathers, eventually becoming one of them. Subsequently, they went to France and we know that John preached to both Alaric and Ataulf. We can assume, therefore, that the marriage of Maria and Ataulf took place about AD 412. Margaret Tottle-Smith's researches indicate that this story is preserved in the archives of the Cassian Foundation in Marseilles. Martin, M., op. cit., p. 44, says that Desposyni had ceased to exist by the seventh century but says, nonetheless, remaining ones joined other rites—Armenian, Syrian, etc., and some reconciled themselves to Rome. He misses the point. Even if, like Cassian, they were reconciled to Rome it did not make them less Desposyni, nor did it stop them from keeping their family's genealogies.

Appendix 1

1. Rhoes the Weoôulgeot

Known as "Rhotestes" in Vit. S. Sabae, Act. SS. Apr.11, 967 D and in the *Orations of Themistics* (Orat. XV, 191A). In the Mercian Kings' List called by the cognomen Weoôulgeot (Ms. Cotton, Vesp. B. VI Fol. 109b, British Museum).

2. Athanaric (Chattaric)

St. Jerome calls him Judge of the Thervingi (Thuringians). He made various treaties with the Emperor Theodosius I. He died in 381 AD at Constantinople. In the Mercian Kings' List called Uihtlag (Woden's Law or Judge).

3. Vermund (Faramund, Pharamond)

Recorded in Mercian Kings' List as son of Uihtlag. *Danish Royal Pedigree* (Langfedgetal) calls him Vermund Vitre (The wise). There is no evidence to prove statements in certain chronicles that Vermund founded the kingdom of the Franks in 425 or that he was the son of Marcomir and father of Hlodio. Still less, that he was elevated on a shield and acclaimed King of the Franks in 420. Gregory and Fredegar do not even mention him. All we can say with certainty is that the Mercian records show him as the son of Uihtlag and we may assume that he succeeded his father in 381 AD.

4. Uffe or Ataulf

The Mercian Kings' List records Uffe or Offa as the son of Vermund. An ancient poem, Wídsíö, calls Offa "the best of all mankind between the seas". As Offa or Uffe is otherwise unknown, it seems likely that the author is referring to Ataulf, the conqueror of Rome together with Alaric. Consider the following:

    i. Ataulf means "The ancestor Ulf or Uffe".

    ii. Uffe is shown as the lineal descendent of Weoôulgeot and King of the Visigoths.

    iii. Ataulf was a lineal descendent of Weoôulgeot and King of the Visigoths and the names are contemporaneous.

    iv. The Elchasaic document shows Maria marrying "Ata" and having a child, Hlodio (or Clodomir).

    v. Uffe is shown as having a child called Hlodio.

vi. Ataulf had two sisters—one married Alaric, King of the Visigoths (Zosima, Historia, Ch. 44 & 45), who died in Italy in 409 and the other married Vallia (Sidonius Appolinaris, carm. II: 360-363, V: 268). Ataulf succeeded his brother-in-law as King of the Visigoths. Some authorities maintain Ataulf and Alaric were brothers, but although it is possible that Alaric married his sister, I personally doubt it. Ataulf was murdered at Barcelona in 415 AD and he was succeeded after a short while by Vallia, his other brother-in-law, who died in Toulouse in 420 AD. Vallia was followed by Theodorid I. Some chroniclers maintain that he was the son of Alaric, which is possible, but Joseph Scaliger calls him "ADAREDE", indicating that he belonged to the ancient royal house of Edom in Syria and Damascus. (See Montgomery, B. G. (1968) – *Ancient Migration and Royal Houses*, p. 115, The Mitre Press, London; see also below, under Scaliger).

vii. John Cassian is known to have preached to Alaric and presumably Ataulf and John had a daughter called Maria.

Joseph Justus Scaliger (1540-1609)

One of the foremost scholars of his day. Converted to Protestantism and became the bane of the Jesuits and the Roman Church. Studied at the College of Guienne in Bordeaux, 1552-1555 and later the University of Paris. Was fluent in Latin, Greek, Hebrew and Arabic. Travelled all over the continent including England and Scotland.

For more information see:

http://en.wikipedia.org/wiki/Joseph_Justus_Scaliger.

Appendix 2

Origins of Documents 1 and 2

When I first published these documents in *Montgomery Millennium* in 2002 I gave an incorrect reference for them. The correct provenance for these documents is as follows:

Joseph Justus Scaliger (1540-1609) was the foremost scholar of his day. He studied at the College of Guienne in Bordeaux and later the University of Paris, first under Turnebus and later under Jean Dorat. It was the latter who recommended Scalinger to Louis de Chastaigner, Lord of La Roche Pozay, with whom he became a lifelong friend and with whom he travelled throughout Europe, studying and buying books and manuscripts.

Scaliger became fluent in Latin, Greek, Hebrew and Arabic and acquired a remarkable collection of original manuscripts in those languages. He also had the opportunity to use the Library of a man named Cujas in Valence, whose library consisted of seven or eight rooms with no less than five hundred original manuscripts.

In 1593 he became Professor at the University of Leiden and remained so for the rest of his life. He became the bane of the Roman Catholic Church and the Jesuits, pointing out to them that many of the books on which they relied were either bogus or at least doubtful. In his *De emendatione temporum* (1583), he revolutionised all the received wisdom on ancient chronology and pointed out that it was necessary to include the chronology of the ancient Persians, Babylonians, Egyptians and Hebrews, hitherto considered worthless.

When he died in 1609 he left all his books and manuscripts to the University Library, including the Leiden Papyrus, dealing with magical spells supposedly used by Jesus (tous mes livres de langues étrangères, Hebraics, Syriens, Arabics, Ethiopiens).

For complete story see *Joseph Scaliger: A Biography*, by Jakob Bernays, Berlin, (1855) or Anthony Grafton – *Joseph Scaliger: A study of Classical Scholarship*, 2 vols. (Oxford Unversity Press, 1983 & 1993). See also: http://en.wikipedia.org./wiki/Joseph_Justus_Scaliger

Document 1 is almost certainly a complete or extended version of St. Mathew's Gospel written in Syria around 150 AD (see Morton Smith's book, *The Secret Gospel of Mark*, p. 142). He discovered a fragment in Greek of the unexpurgated version, which has been authenticated.

William Montgomery (1633-1706) also played a role in these documents. He was educated at the University of Leiden where he studied Latin, Greek and Hebrew. He translated two of these documents into English (Documents 3 and 4) using an English not dissimilar to the Authorised Version of the Bible. These versions he kept and later put them into the Library of County Down, Ireland, when appointed "Custos Rotulorum" by the Duke of Ormonde. It is also quite likely that he translated the following Document 1 fragment.

Original English Version of Document 1

And David the King begat Solomon on the wife of Uriah the Hittite and Solomon begat Roboam, who begat Abia ....(it goes on in this vein with several fragments missing until)—And Jacob begat on ...Joseph who begat on his wife Miriam, Jeshua, Judah and Jacob and Jeshua begat on his wife Miriam of Bethany (of the house) of Saul, a daughter ....and on Mirium... (of the house of) Æthiopia a son.....and (a daughter)...and Joseph of the House of Arimathea begat on...

The parts in brackets are my interpretation, not William's.

One of the most ancient Orthodox Churches is that of Cyprus. According to the Curator of the Archbishop Makarios Museum, the Apostle Barnabas (Vanabas in Greek) had died on the Island in 58 AD and was the founder of the Cypriot Church. In 588 AD they discovered his body and upon disinterment found that he had been buried with a much mildewed copy of the "complete" Gospel of Mathew in Hebrew. They are quite definite that it was in Hebrew and predated the later Greek version. This document was taken to Constantinople and on every Maunday Thursday (a feast day in the Roman Catholic and Anglican calendars) the Emperor would read the beginning of the Gospel from his throne in the Haga Sophia. According to a book on Byzantium, at the end of this reading the Emperor would proclaim, "From whom we (The Emperor) are descended." The choir then chanted "Kyrie Eleison". I do not know, or at least have been unable to ascertain, whether the Emperor read out from the Hebrew original or a Greek copy.

In 1439 the then Emperor, John Paleologos, went to Italy to try to heal the rift between the Orthodox and Roman Catholic Church. This venture failed because of Rome's intransigence. It was recorded at the time that amongst the gifts brought by the Emperor was a copy of the Gospel of St. Mathew. Cosimo de Medici had the General Council transferred from Ferrara to Florence and had himself elected *Gonfaloniere* for the occasion of the Emperor's entry into Florence. He also took the occasion of so many Greek scholars, being in Florence, to establish his academy of Platonic studies in Florence under the influence of John Argyropoulos and Marsilio Ficino. It would appear also that many of the documents brought with the Imperial delegation finished up in Cosimo's Library. (See *The Rise and Fall of the House of Medici*, by C. Hibbert (1974), Penguin, pp. 65-69.) Some two hundred years later some of these documents had found their way into the Library of Cujas in Valence.

It seems likely, therefore, that this may be the origin of the unexpurgated version of Mathew which, according to Prof. Morton Smith, also existed in Syriac.

Document 1 and at least part of Document 2, probably as far down as the Two Marthas, almost certainly had their origin as part of the submissions of what I have called the Anti-Niceane Fathers (to distinguish them from the Ante-Nicene Fathers) in AD 325 at the Council of Nicaea. This group, who probably included members of Jesus' family, objected to Jesus being made 'Divine'. They produced as part of their submission a genealogy of Jesus' descendents and posed the question, "If Jesus is divine are his children divine?"

The Church decided instead to expunge all reference to Jesus' descendents and came up with the clumsy explanation of the Trinity. The tradition of the Anti-Niceane Fathers is carried on today by the Unitarians and of course by Islam, which denies Jesus' divinity.

Appendix 3

1. *The Gospel of the Essenes* has been translated from the original Hebrew and Aramaic texts by Edmond Bordeaux Szekely and is published by C.W. Daniel Co., Ltd., Saffron Walden, UK. It was first published in 1974.

2. The Gospel of Mary was discovered in Cairo in 1896, some fifty years before the Nag Hammadi Scrolls. It was left in the care of the Berlin Museum and the first translation was not done until 1955. It is now available in English as *The Gospel of Mary Magdelene*, translated from French by Jean-Yves Leloup and published by Inner Traditions International, Vermont, USA. In my opinion it should be called, as the original Coptic text suggests, *The Gospel of Mary*. See page 40 of this edition. The original, like the Gospel of Thomas, is written in Sahidic Coptic, though there exists a fragment in Greek, which predates but confirms the Coptic version (Rylands Papyrus 463). Document 4 is from the same source.

3. The Nag Hammadi Scrolls were first found in 1945 at Nag Hammadi near Phou in Egypt. This includes the Gospel of Thomas, dating originally to circa 50 AD and thought to be contemporaneous with the "Q" text, the missing source for the canonical Gospels.

4. Mary Magdelene's identification with prostitution stems from Homily 33 of Pope Gregory I in 591 when this Pope declared, "She whom Luke calls the sinful woman, whom John calls Mary, we believe to be the Mary from whom seven devils were ejected according to Mark. And what did these seven devils signify, if not all the vices?... It is clear, brothers, that the woman previously used the unguent to perfume her flesh in forbidden acts." It has been quite clear to scholars for a long time now that Pope Gregory was wrong. *There is no reference anywhere in the gospels to Mary being a prostitute.* In fact, in 1969 the Catholic Church repealed Pope Gregory's error.

5. Another non-canonical Gospel, the *Gospel of Philip*, states quite specifically that Jesus was married. "There were three who always walked with the Lord: Mary his mother; the sister of his mother and Miriam of Magdala, known as his companion (koinonos). For him Miriam is a sister, a mother and a wife." The word *Koinonos* is used in both cases. This indicates quite clearly that they are sexually intimate. Indeed, the Gospel makes clear that Jesus kissed her on the lips. Unthinkable unless they

were married. Some scholars will argue over whether Jesus kissed her "on the lips" or on some other part of her anatomy. As she was his sexual partner, it is likely that he kissed her on many parts of her body. The argument is, of course, a bit esoteric and much like the medieval argument over how many angels could dance on the head of a pin. There is another interesting point. "The sister of his mother" may not mean Aunt, as some scholars have suggested, but it might mean his sister by his mother (i.e. half-sister), suggesting that Mary, his mother, may have been married previously. It is indeed possible that Mary was married to Joseph's elder brother, Jacob, but that her first husband died before any children were born and that she and Joseph then performed a Levirate Marriage—whereby the brother of a widow, whose husband died without heirs, married the widow and the first born is the heir of the brother. In this case it is likely that Mary-Jacob, Jesus' sister, was the first-born and called Mary-Jacob, to show that she was the daughter of Joseph's brother, Jacob (see Schneid, H. (1973) – *Marriage*, p. 49, Keter Books, Jerusalem).

6. The latest translation of the Gospel of Thomas by Leloup reads: "These are the words of the Secret. They were revealed by the living Yeshua. Didymus Judas Thomas wrote them down." Leloup, Jean-Yves (1986) – *The Gospel of Thomas*, p. 9, Inner Traditions, Rochester, Vermont, USA. His actual name was Judas or Judah. Thomas and Didymus both mean twin. Thomas comes from the Hebrew *TEUM*, and Didymus is Greek for twin. They were revealed by the *LIVING JESUS*, not a resurrected Jesus, and they are *SECRET*.

7. On p. 121 of the Gospel of Philip, above referenced, it states:

"Those who say that we first die and are then resurrected are wrong. Whoever is not resurrected before death knows nothing and will die."

"The tree of life lives in the middle of another garden. It is the olive tree from which the oil of anointment is drawn. Thanks to it, resurrection is possible."

8. The Acts of Thomas are part of the Apocrypha. It says Judas Thomas is the author. He is the twin of Jesus and looks like him (Chap. 11). He is the holder of secret knowledge. The Acts of Thomas form the oldest

documents in the possession of the Syrian Church where the concept of Jesus having a twin was always accepted. Indeed, most of the Middle Eastern Churches originally accepted this without question (see *Apocrypha*, p. 442). I have also used the German translation (*Neu Testamentich Apokrythen*, Vol. 2, translated by E. Hennecke & W. Schneemelcher, 4th edition, 1968) and which has a slightly different emphasis on some matters than the English. The Acts probably originated in Edessa during the early part of the 3rd century (220-250 AD) but fragments of an original Greek version exist. (Lake, K., *A Fragment of the Acta Thomae in texts from Mount Athos* (Oxford, 1903). For those interested, I give below the texts to which they can refer:

a. Greek

Thilo, C., *Acta S. Thomae Apostoli* (Leipzig, 1823), 4 MSS.
Tischendorf, C., *Acta Apostolorum Apocrypha* (Leipzig, 1851, 190-230, 5 MSS plus 2 further MSS, Apocalypses Apocryphae.
Lake, K., mentioned above.

b. Syriac

I. Wright, *Apoc. Acts*, i. 171-333; ii (English Translation).

II. Bedjan, P., *Acta Martyrum et Sanctorum*, iii (Paris & Leipzig, 1892, reproduced by Hildesheim, 1968).

III. Burkitt, F. C., *Fragments of the Acts of Judas Thomas from the Sinaitic Palimpsest in Select Narratives of Holy Women* (London, 1900), App. VII.

IV. Ortiz de Urbana, I., *Patrologica Syriaca* (Rome, 1965).

There are also Latin Translations.

Appendix 4
Notes for Family of Jesus from All Sources genealogical charts 1 & 2

a. See Mark 2:14, John 3:1-7, John 19:39.

b. See Thiering, B., *Jesus the Man op. cit.* pp. 392, 80, 72, 232, 107, 220, 231, 98, 111, 115, 217, 131, 133, 254, 339, 134, 255, 152, 284 also Acts 6:5 & 18:95.

c. See under Simon Magus & Simon the Leper, Thiering, B., op. cit pp. 78-263; also Fitzmayer, J. A. (1971) – *Essays on the Semitic background of the New Testament*, pp. 447-460, London. Also John 11:1-6 & 43, Acts 8:9-10.

d. See Luke 10:38-42, John 11:1, 24, 27 & 12:1-8.

e. The marriage of Mary of Bethany and Jesus is shown in the Gospel of Philip, op. cit., p. 65, John 2:9-10 also Thiering, op. cit., p. 148. Also Documents 1 & 2 mentioned in text believed to be the unexpurgated version of Mathew and a genealogy prepared on the instruction of Chlodimir. Mary is also mentioned in John 11:20, 12:3, 20:1-5. The marriage of Jesus is also shown in Eusebius, op. cit., Chap. 3 by implication.

f. Jesus & Miriam's first child was a daughter called Miriam after her mother, however, she is also called Sarah. Sarah is a title meaning Princess, but was also the title used by the female Bishop of Ephesus. She is also called Tamar or Damaris. Damar is a Greek word meaning wife and the "is" at the end would be its genitive form, however, according to the *Oxford Dictionary of Proper Names*, this may be a mistake for (or in place of) Damalis, meaning young girl. See Documents 1 & 2; also Acts 3:20-21 & 17:34; also Thiering, B., op. cit., p. 151. Also Julius Africanus and Eusebius. Sigismundus is only known from the Elchasaic genealogy. Thiering suggests that she married Paul.

g. Some authorities have called him Jeshua II, but this is not possible as his father was still alive and under Jewish convention a son was not named after his father unless his father was dead. He would, however, have been called Ben Yeshua. See Acts 6:7, 1:23: 18:9. Also Thiering, op. cit., April, AD 44, p. 262.

h. See Acts 12:24 & Rev. 2:17.

i. Jesus' daughter by Miriam of Bethany was also called Miriam after her mother. She would also have been called Sarah, which was simply a title, meaning Princess. So she would have been known as Sarah Miriam. Just as, for example, Princess Anne's name is Anne and her title Princess. Upon becoming an adult at about 14 she would also have become known as Demalis (Greek for unmarried woman) and would have become known as Demalis Sarah Miriam. Again, compare this with Princess Anne at age 14 becoming HRH. Upon her marriage to Saul she would have changed her title to Demaris (Greek for "wife of") and became Demaris Sarah Miriam. Saul was not of the Davidic blood, but by marrying Miriam (the Eldest daughter and heir presumptive because the eldest son was not yet of Royal Age), he had to assume the position of protector of the Davidic Line (anointed, as in "Christus"). He therefore changed his name to Paul.

In Greek, Christ was usually shown as the Greek letters, and if you take the P and substitute it for the first letter of Saul's name you get Paul. There was also another coded title that each held. In the case of Miriam this was in Greek, Phoibus, or Latin, Phoebus (in the English Bible it is usually Phoebe), meaning "The Bright or Pure One". In the case of Paul it was "The Sign to the World", or Sigismundus (from the Latin "Sigilis" and "Mundus"). Thus, the Bright or Pure One married the Sign to the World, the person whose work would bring "Christianity" to the world and whose line became the senior Davidic/Saulic Line.

j. Alanus or Alain is found in the 14th century *Estoire del Saint Graal* on p. 120, published in 1861, trans. By H. L. Skymer.

k. *The Questre del St. Graal*, trans. Matarasso, Penguin, 1976. Also Alanus.

l. Both the son and Ruth are to be found in Document 2, c. 416 AD, and in Thiering.

m. Mentioned in a letter from Eleutherius to King Lucius, c. 190 AD, and quoted in *The Coming of the Saints*, by J. Taylor, Covenant Books, 1969.

n. Elchasai—mentioned in Document 2; also in Yuri Stoyanov's book, *The Hidden Tradition in Europe*, also in Codex Mani and a number of other sources mentioned in the text.

o. Both mentioned in Document 2 and also by Yuri Stoyanov. Further references are to be found in the text.

p. Maria's father preached to both Alaric and Ataulf somewhere between 410-412 AD and against Athanasius. It is probable that she came to Ataulf's attention then and they were probably married about 412 AD. Ataulf did not have children by Galla Placidia.

q. As Ataulf is known not to have had children by Galla Placidia it may reasonably be inferred that Clodomir was his child by Maria.

r. See text for details.

s. Jacob & Heli – Mathew 1:18, Luke 3:23. Esther, Jacob's wife, had previously been married to his brother Heli and then, according to Eusebius, contracted a levirate marriage to Jacob. By blood they would be Jacob's children, but legally they would be Heli's. Modern scholars tend to maintain that Eusebius was merely producing this explanation for the discrepancies between Mathew and Luke, but our researches have found a number of levirate marriages and we think Eusebius was correct.

t. Joachim and Hanna—The protoevangelism of James in *The Apocryphal New Testament*, p. 51.

u. Miriam—Document 1, Luke 1:26 & 1:56, John Chaps. 2, 3 & 5 etc., Gospel of Philip, op. cit. p. 65.

v. A non-Jewish wife – I could only find one rather vague reference to this in Max Dimont's *Jews, God & History*. The Idumeans were conquered and converted to Judaism forcibly by John Hycarnus. Herod's family were of this line. However, not all Idumeans accepted Judaism, including some of Herod's family. It is likely, therefore, that Joseph's second wife was one of these. However, Malachi Martin, Jesuit Professor in Rome, says on page 43 of his book, *The Decline and Fall of the Roman Church* (G. P. Putnam & Sons, New York, 1981), "There were, of course, numerous blood descendents of Joseph, Mary's husband,..." but as he considers them not begotten of Mary, logically, Joseph had another wife.

w. Salome and Dorcas were both born in 18 AD making them twins. It seems to run in the family. See Mark 16:1; Mark 16:40; Acts 9:40; Acts 9:36 & 9:39; also Morton Smith's *The Secret Gospel of Mark*.

x. Simon or Simeon—Mark 5:3; Acts 10:6.

y. Philip the uncircumcised—This is our principle reason for believing that Joseph's second wife was non-Jewish, as otherwise he would be circumcised. It is possible, however, that he was a "bleeder" or haemophiliac and his parents were given permission for the child not to be circumcised, but we think then that this would have been mentioned somewhere. Mark 3:18; Luke 6:14; Acts 8: 26-40.

z. Jeshua & Judah were twins born in 7 BC. Judah is called both Thomas and Didymus, both of which mean twin—*Gospel of Thomas, op. cit.*, p. 9. Mathew 13:55; Mark 1:19, 3:17, 5:3 & 10:35 (Jacob); also Mark 15:40, 5:3 & 15:47 (Josiah). For Joanna, see Mark 5:3 & Luke 5:3. For Mary-Jacob, see Mark 5:3.

aa. Mary Magdelene—Barbara Thiering calls her Lydia but I suggest that "from Lydia" or "the Lydian" might be more correct. Certainly Document 1 calls her Mirium. She had, according to both Document 1 and Barbara Thiering, two children by Jesus—Joseph, born 28 AD, and Ruth, who, like her mother, was called the Lydian in 57 AD.

ABDIAE
BABYLONIAE PRIMI
EPISCOPI AB APOSTOLIS
CONSTITVTI, DE HISTORIA
certaminis Apostolici, Libri X.

IVLIO AFRICANO interprete.

B. Matthiæ Apostoli, Marci, Clementis, Cypriani, &
Apollinaris vita, ex scriniis primitiuæ Eccle-
siæ Notariorum deprompta.

Vita B. Martini Sabariensis, Turonensis Episcopi,
à Seuero Sulpitio conscripta.

Quæ nunquam hactenus excussa prodeunt.

S. Marcialis discipuli Domini vita ab Aureliano quem
idé sibi Episcopú Lemouicésem substituit, descripta.

S. *Martini Turonensis Episcopi fidei Confessio, breuibus scho-*
liis à F. Thoma Beauxamis illustrata.

PARISIIS,
Apud Thomam Belot sub D. Barbaræ
signo, in via Iacobæa.

1571.
CVM PRIVILEGIO.

Title page to the Abdias Manuscript (courtesy of the Norris Collection, Dickinson College)

Appendix 5

Just before this book was published I received a photocopy of the only known complete Abdias manuscript, courtesy of the Norris collection. It is beautifully produced and although printed in 1571, appears to be a faithful copy of the original manuscript in the Hapsburg collection.

Abdias was the first Bishop of Babylonia and is supposed to be one of the 70 or 72 disciples of Jesus. He wrote 10 sermons, one on each of the Apostles, in Hebrew. These were translated into Greek and then later into Latin by Julius Africanos. There is some indication that Abdias may have been a member of Jesus' family and certainly he claims to know various members of the family.

The Catholic Church, of course, claim that he was Apocryphal and that the book was written by a French Monk in the 6th century. There are a number of interesting reasons why this cannot possibly be true:

1. He is mentioned by Eusebius, the Church historian, in his book written in 306 AD.

2. Eusebius mentions the Latin text of Julius Africanos and says that it was produced prior to 200 AD.

3. The Latin is the rather better Latin of the first and second century AD and not the far more clumsy Latin of later dates when Latin was no longer a spoken language.

In the Latin version the following interesting texts appear:

1. Liber Nonus: "Beatum Thomam...ipsumque a Domino Didymum, quod interpretatur geminus." This translates as: Book Nine: "The Blessed Thomas...himself Didymus to the Lord, which is to be interpreted as *his twin*." Further in the Acts of Thomas it states that he was Jesus' identical twin. This makes the immaculate conception difficult, to put it mildly.

2. Julius also translates the Greek word "Desposyni" as "Progenies et cognate a Domino" (Latin), which then translates as, "The descendents (progeny) and relatives to the Lord."

Index

Printed in the United States
79495LV00003B/75